J.M.W. Turner

Ashmolean handbooks

J.M.W. Turner

Luke Herrmann and Colin Harrison

Published with the aid of a
generous grant from

SPINK-LEGER
PICTURES

Ashmolean Museum Oxford
2000

ISBN 1 85444 122 1 (papercased)
ISBN 1 85444 121 3 (paperback)

Titles in this series include:
Ruskin's drawings
Worcester porcelain
Maiolica
Drawings by Michelangelo and Raphael
Oxford and the Pre-Raphaelites
Islamic ceramics
Indian paintings from Oxford collections
Camille Pissarro and his family
Eighteenth-century French porcelain
Miniatures
Samuel Palmer
Twentieth century paintings
Ancient Greek pottery
English Delftware
Glass of four millennia

British Library Cataloguing in Publication Data
A catalogue record for this book is available from the British Library

Cover illustration: *Blois*, no. 28

Designed and typeset in Versailles by Roy Cole, Wells
Printed and bound in the United Kingdom by Balding + Mansell Limited, Norwich

Introduction

The recent long-term loan of three early oil paintings from the Loyd Collection, together with the more than eighty drawings and watercolours and the fine representation of *Liber Studiorum* prints, make it possible to see an outstanding group of work by J.M.W. Turner (1775–1851) at the Ashmolean Museum. This handbook provides a selection arranged in chronological order, and gives a brief account of their acquisition and of the history of Turner's work on paper.

The first examples of Turner's work to enter the Ashmolean (then known as the University Galleries) were the ten watercolours engraved and published as headpieces of the Oxford Almanack between 1799 and 1811, and deposited by the Delegates of the Clarendon Press in 1850. The first two drawings, one of which is reproduced here as no. 7, were commissioned from Turner in 1798, when he was only twenty-three, but already considered one of the leading topographical watercolour artists of the day.

The majority of the Turner drawings at Oxford were presented to his old University by John Ruskin (1819–1900), the artist's great champion and interpreter in his final years, who, at first with the financial help of his father, formed an unrivalled collection of his hero's work. Ruskin's first presentation of Turner drawings to Oxford was in March 1861, when he gave fifty drawings. These included twelve early black chalk drawings, mostly of views around Eton, now no longer attributed to Turner (Herrmann 11–22). Two months later, Ruskin presented a group of twenty-five Turner drawings to the Fitzwilliam Museum in Cambridge. He continued to collect the work of Turner, and when, soon after his appoinment as Slade Professor of Fine Art at Oxford in 1869, he founded the Ruskin School of Drawing, the drawings, prints, photographs and reproductions he assembled as 'Series of Examples' for the students, included a considerable group of Turner drawings. The twenty-eight examples he finally selected complemented the works in the 1861 gift to provide in Oxford an overall survey of Turner's work as a draughtsman. Since then, six drawings by Turner and a small group of drawings formerly attributed to him have been added to the collection. It was only in 1997 that the loan of the three Loyd Collection Turners (nos. 13, 15 and 16) has made it possible also to see paintings by him in Oxford.

To store and display his gifts, Ruskin provided beautifully designed and constructed mahogany cabinets containing the drawings in frames that slid in and out. He had provided similar cases for the National Gallery for the exhibition of drawings from the Turner Bequest, the sorting of which he had supervised in the winter of 1857–8. Some years later, Ruskin persuaded the Trustees of the National Gallery to sanction the loan to Oxford University of some 250 drawings and sketches from the Turner Bequest; these remained on exhibition in Oxford from 1879 to 1906.

In the Introduction to his *Notes* accompanying the exhibition of his own Turner drawings at the Fine Art Society in Bond Street in 1878, John Ruskin divided Turner's development as a draughtsman into decades, starting in 1790 when the artist was fifteen. Between 1790 and 1800, Turner studied at the Royal Academy Schools and with the architectural draughtsman Thomas Malton the Younger and others. During this period Turner was carefully studying the work of his British predecessors and contemporaries, some of which he copied, especially when working in Dr Monro's 'Academy'. The first seven reproductions in this handbook represent these years: *Boats on a Beach* (no. 2), dating from 1793, and the unfinished *The Ruined Abbey at Headington* (no. 4), of a year or two later, provide valuable insight into the precise and effective working methods of the young artist, who was still in his teens. No. 5, *'Transept of Tintern Abbey, Monmouthshire'*, which was purchased by the Ashmolean in 1917, may have been one of the eight watercolours that Turner exhibited at the Royal Academy in 1795, and is a fine example of his carefully composed and picturesque exhibition pieces of this time. In 1796 Turner showed his first oil painting at the Royal Academy, as well as ten watercolours, and two years later he was elected an Associate. The final example from this decade is the first of the watercolours Turner made in 1798 to be engraved as the headpieces for the Oxford Almanack (no. 7).

During the second decade, 1800–1810, which is represented here by five drawings (nos. 8–10, 12 and 14) and the first two Loyd paintings (nos. 13 and 15), Turner consolidated his position as the leading topographical watercolour artist of the day, and established his reputation as a painter in oils; he was elected R.A. in 1802. He was also moving towards the more personal style which came to the fore in the following decade, but which can already be seen in the painting, *Walton Bridges*, of about 1806, in which the bridges of the title actually play a secondary role. For his later Oxford Almanack drawings Turner retained the traditional topographical style of the first two, as is shown by those reproduced here, and the oil painting of the *View of the High Street, Oxford* is painted in a similar manner. Turner's growing interest in 'pure' landscape is demonstrated by the fine pencil drawing enhanced by some watercolour, *Distant View of Lowther Castle – Park Scene,* one of three studies in the Ruskin School Collection for Turner's two paintings of the Earl of Lonsdale's recently built Lowther Castle, in Westmoreland, which the artist had visited in the summer of 1809.

Thanks largely to the gifts of John Ruskin there is an important collection of Turner's *Liber Studiorum* prints in the Ashmolean, one of which, *Lake of Thun* (no. 11), published in 1808, is reproduced here. The earliest drawing from the third decade, 1810–20, the pen and wash *Study of Trees* (no. 17), is associated with the *Liber* mezzotint *Berry Pomeroy Castle* (Finberg 58), published in Part XII in 1816. There are three other drawings (nos. 18–20) from this decade, during which Turner's mastery of the medium of watercolour became complete, though he largely stopped exhibiting watercolours, and his palette grew much lighter and more colourful. *Sunshine on the Tamar,* with its wonderful combination of quite elaborate foreground detail, including the famous pigs, and hazy landscape in the distance, dates from about 1813 and is an outstanding example of Turner's fluent and effective use of watercolours at this time. The final Loyd canvas, *Whalley Bridge and Abbey, Lancashire,* is an evocation of rural tranquillity. It was shown at the Royal Academy in 1811, but was surprisingly ignored by the critics for whom Turner's exhibits were usually of prime interest by now.

The remaining two drawings from the third decade are both associated with Farnley Hall, the Yorkshire seat of Turner's foremost early patron and great friend, Walter Fawkes. From 1810 until Fawkes's death in 1825, Turner was a frequent and welcome visitor at Farnley, where he made numerous drawings and watercolours of the house, its contents and its surroundings. *A Frontispiece (at Farnley Hall),* in which the house is seen in the background, was drawn as the frontispiece to a set of drawings, still at Farnley, illustrating the collection of 'Fairfaxiana' – relics of the Cromwellian general, Thomas Fairfax – belonging to Fawkes. Another Yorkshire subject is the *Junction of the Greta and the Tees at Rokeby,* which Ruskin considered the best of his Oxford Turner drawings and to which he made frequent references in his lectures and writings. This dates from about 1818, and was engraved in 1819 on a reduced scale by John Pye, as one of the plates for Dr Whitaker's *History of Richmondshire,* for which Turner made twenty watercolours. Some of the finest plates yet produced of his work were engraved for this series.

During the fourth decade, 1820–30, Turner's colour and handling became ever more confident, and his own individual style was achieved.

The largest group of Ruskin's Turners belongs to this decade, represented here by nos. 21–29. Many of these were made for engraving, as were the majority of Turner's finished watercolour drawings of this period. The earliest of these here is the lively composition of *Comb Martin (Devonshire)*, which dates from about 1824 and was engraved by William Miller, one of Turner's favourite younger engravers, for Cooke's *Picturesque Views on the Southern Coast of England*, and published in 1826. The sparkling *Sketch of Mackerel*, which Ruskin rightly considered largely a study of colour, and the rapid study of *Yarmouth, Norfolk*, demonstrating Turner's lifelong fascination with the movement and moods of the sea, are both more private works, in almost pure watercolour with very little pencil drawing. There is no evidence of pencil outlines in the equally spontaneous *Margate (Kent)*, which is notable for the powerful blue of the sea. It was engraved in mezzotint in about 1828 by Thomas Lupton for his *Ports of England*, though the plate was not published until 1856, when it was one of twelve in *The Harbours of England by Turner and Ruskin*, published by Ernest Gambart with an introduction and comments on each plate by Ruskin, containing what has been described as 'the finest writing on the sea in the English language'.

The nucleus of Ruskin's 1861 gift was the group of twenty-four drawings connected with the famous 'Rivers of France' series published in three volumes as *Turner's Annual Tour* from 1833 to 1835 (nos. 25–29 and 31). The first volume was devoted to the Loire, and seventeen of the twenty drawings engraved for this are in Oxford; the other two volumes illustrated the Seine. Ruskin had only acquired these precious drawings, which he had long coveted, in 1858, when he bought them from Mrs Hannah Cooper, who had inherited them in 1853 from her uncle Charles Stokes, Turner's friend and stockbroker and a considerable Turner collector, especially of the *Liber Studiorum*. These jewel-like compositions, drawn in watercolour and body colour on small sheets of fairly rough paper that were originally blue, but faded to grey even before Ruskin acquired them, combine assured recording of detail with superb rendering of atmosphere. They were based on numerous rapid pencil studies made by Turner on his painstaking tours of the rivers undertaken during several summers in the later 1820s and early 1830s. The colourful finished drawings were brilliantly engraved on steel by a group of engravers, many of whom had been schooled by Turner, who always kept a very close eye on the engraving of his drawings.

In the fifth decade of his career, 1830–40, Turner continued to produce numerous drawings for engraving, many of them small, minutely detailed vignettes designed to illustrate various literary works, of which there are two examples in Ruskin's gift of 1861. Many of these were of places never visited by Turner and were based on sketches by other artists, like the small and precise drawing of *Jericho* (no. 30), which dates from about 1835. This was based on a sketch by the Revd R. Masters and engraved on steel by William Finden for *The Biblical Keepsake*, published by John Murray in 1835. Ruskin owned six of the drawings for what came to be known as 'Finden's Bible', and particularly admired these, describing them 'as quite unrivalled examples of his [Turner's] richest power on a small scale'.

During these same years, as also in the final decade of his career, Turner was producing hundreds of wonderfully fluent and sparkling watercolour studies, many of them on a large scale, to record specific light and colour effects or to develop ideas for compositions. These are in stark contrast to the highly finished vignette drawings and were essentially 'private' works. The great majority remained in his studio and form part of the so-called 'Turner Bequest' to the National Gallery, now housed in the Clore Gallery at the Tate Gallery. Turner was also making relatively small numbers of 'finished' watercolours for sale – in particular the great series of Swiss watercolours executed between 1842 and 1845 and based on numerous watercolour studies made on the spot during his annual summer visits to Switzerland from 1841 to 1844. Ruskin commissioned and acquired several of these, which he rightly considered to be the greatest watercolours by Turner, and therefore the most wonderful of all English watercolours. None of these finished watercolours were included in his gifts, but there is a small group of late studies in the Ruskin School Collection, including the vivid *Evening: Cloud on Mont Rigi, seen from Zug* (no. 34). In this, Turner did not use any pencil, and left large areas of the paper bare to produce effects of light and reflection. These studies illustrate Turner's wonderful dexterity with the medium, frequently applied in unorthodox ways, including the use of fingers and thumb.

Turner's latest works in Oxford are the three beautiful Venetian watercolours, of which two are reproduced here – nos. 32 and 33. Turner visited Venice at least three times, the last in the late summer of 1840, and it is now thought that the many late Venetian studies all date from this final visit. Taken as a whole, these fluent watercolours provide the most engrossing survey of the unique character, atmosphere and light of Venice, where both Ruskin and Turner were in their element. While in *Venice: the Grand Canal* there is little actual watercolour and the composition largely relies on the use of pen with red and blue ink, and wash for the focal gondola, there is more watercolour in *Venice: the Accademia*, though here again the work with pen in red and black ink is an essential element of the composition. It is not known how much of these Venetian studies was actually drawn on the spot, and it seems possible that Turner used just watercolour while working in the open, and applied the pen and ink later in the day when he had returned to the Hotel Europa on the Grand Canal, where he was staying.

Thanks to John Ruskin, the Ashmolean Museum has the finest and most representative public English collection of Turner's watercolours and drawings outside London. In the 140 or so years since Ruskin made his gifts to the University Turner's posthumous reputation has never diminished, and since the bicentenary of his birth in 1975 it has greatly increased. Since then numerous exhibitions and publications in most parts of the world have made his work available to an ever larger audience. Ruskin's pioneering gifts of representative collections to Oxford and Cambridge can be seen as an early factor in maintaining Turner's reputation, for which his own writings, especially *Modern Painters*, were, of course, even more important.

Luke Herrmann

Chronology

23 April 1775	Joseph Mallord William Turner born in Maiden Lane, Covent Garden
11 December 1789	entered Royal Academy Schools
1790	first watercolours exhibited at Royal Academy
1793	awarded 'Great Silver Palette' of Royal Society of Arts for landscape drawing
1794	probably began to frequent Dr Thomas Monro's evening classes, copying works by J.R. Cozens and others
1796	first oil painting exhibited at Royal Academy
1799	elected Associate of Royal Academy; first watercolour for Oxford Almanack reproduced (no. 7)
1802	elected full member of Royal Academy
1807	publication of first instalment of *Liber Studiorum* (see no. 11); elected Professor of Perspective at R.A.
1808	stayed with Sir John Leicester at Tabley (no. 13)
1810	first stayed with Walter Fawkes of Farnley (no. 19)
1811	tour of West Country in connexion with *The Southern Coast* (no. 23)
1817	first tour of Belgium, North Germany and Holland
[1819	birth of John Ruskin]
1820	first tour of Italy
1826	tour of Meuse, Moselle, Loire
1828	second visit to Italy
1831	tour of Scotland
1833	visited Paris
1836	Ruskin's first letter to Turner
1840	visited Venice (nos. 32–3); met Ruskin for first time
1841, 1842, 1844	in Switzerland (see no. 34)
19 December 1851	died at home in Cheyne Walk. Buried at St Paul's Cathedral, 30 December

Bibliographical abbreviations
(see page 80 for full details)

Butlin and Joll	Martin Butlin and Evelyn Joll, *The Paintings of J.M.W. Turner*
Herrmann	Luke Herrmann, *Ruskin and Turner*
Petter	Helen Mary Petter, *The Oxford Almanacks*
Powell	Cecilia Powell, *Turner's Rivers of Europe*
Rawlinson	W.G. Rawlinson, *The Engraved Work of J.M.W. Turner*
Wilton	Andrew Wilton, *The Life and Work of J.M.W. Turner*

Turner Bequest, catalogued in A.J. Finberg, *A Complete Inventory of the Turner Bequest*

1 *Craig-y-foel, Radnorshire*

watercolours over pencil, touched with the reed pen in black ink, 16.7 × 20.9 cm
signed in ink, lower right, *W. Turner*
inscribed on a separate sheet in pencil by Turner, *Near Rhaidder*; and in ink in contemporary hands, *Drawing by Turner / at his 1st Visit to Hereford / in his way to Rayder & / the Devils Bridge / 24th June 1792 / a present 1 Originale Sketch / W. M. Turner Craggy Voyle in Breconshire near the River Ellon*
Bequeathed by the Revd Robert Finch to the Taylor Institution, 1830 and transferred thence, 1913 [1913.9]
Herrmann 88; Wilton 29

The mountains and valleys of Wales had attracted artists in search of the primeval and the picturesque since the early eighteenth century, and the publication of William Gilpin's *Observations on the River Wye . . . made in the summer of 1770* (London, 1782), was both symptomatic of the popularity of such tours, and stimulated their further success. Turner's first tour followed the route consecrated by Gilpin up the Wye Valley as far as the Devil's Bridge. From the numerous pencil sketches he made on the tour, Turner worked up several watercolours. As the inscription suggests, the rather unpromising subject of this drawing is a small group of houses in the Elan valley, not far from Rhayader, now submerged. The trees and grass in the foreground, roughly drawn in pen and black ink, frame the brightly lit houses and the majestic mountains almost billow up like clouds behind. The large signature is characteristic of the work of the young artist seeking to make his reputation.

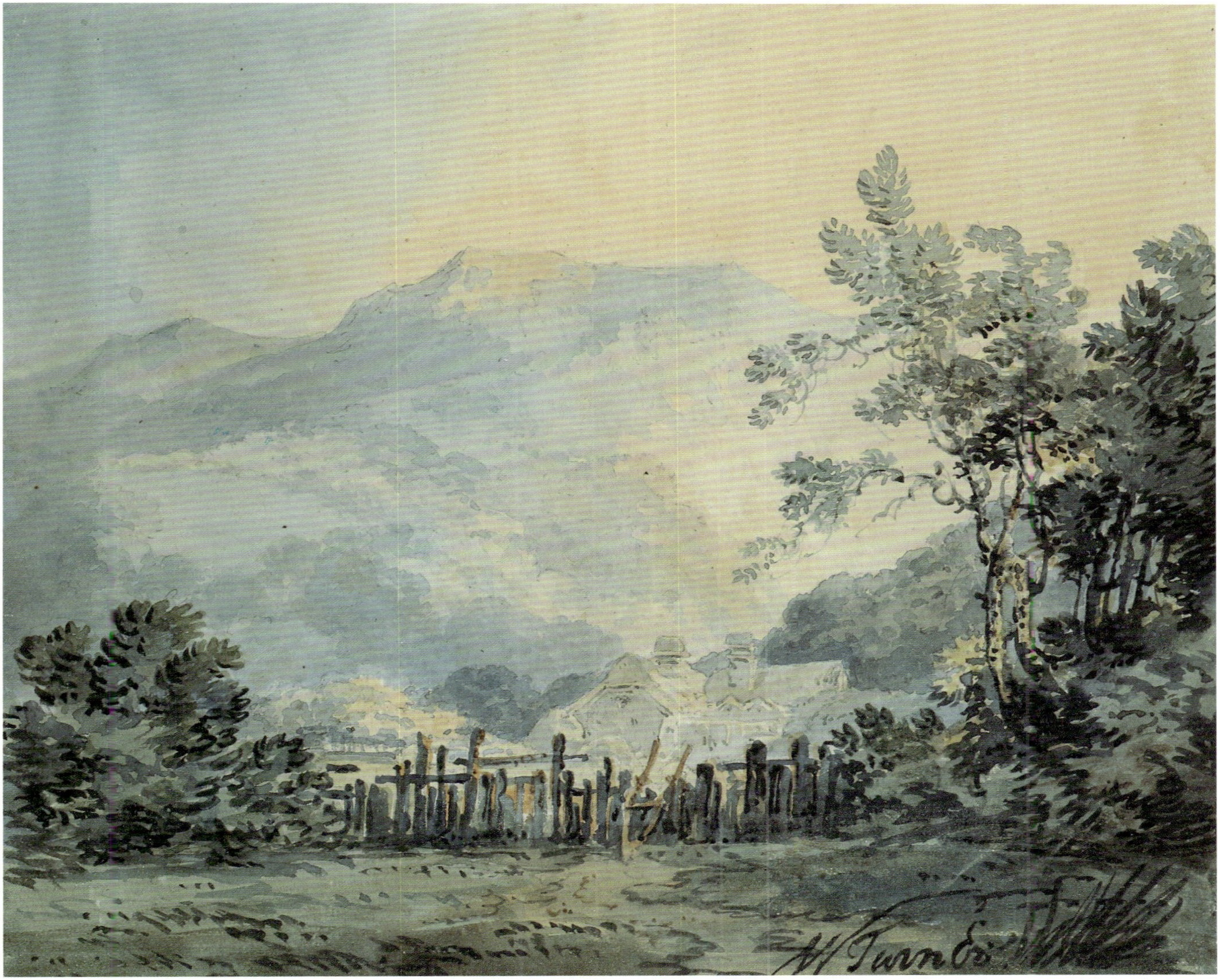
W Turner

2 *Boats on a Beach*

watercolours over pencil, 13.1 × 21.6 cm
Ruskin School Collection (Rudimentary Series, no. 126)
Herrmann 59

In *c.*1792, Turner joined the drawing school run by the alienist[1] Dr Thomas Monro, copying the watercolours of John Robert Cozens; among his fellow pupils were Thomas Girtin and Edward Dayes. Turner also studied with Monro's friend and neighbour, John Henderson, who used his own drawings and those of Canaletto as models. *Boats on a Beach* is one of a series of drawings in pencil and watercolour associated with Henderson, and was presumably copied from one of Henderson's own drawings, though this has not been traced.

Ruskin described this drawing as a 'study, of consummate excellence, in Turner's early manner', of the

> utmost delicacy, with utmost decision. Take a lens to it, you will find the teeth of the saw in the carpenter's hand, and the blocks of the shrouds, in the distant vessels. Yet the gradation of the interior of the boat is given with one dash of colour, carefully managed while wet, and the harmony of the whole is perfect. The sky is singularly tender and lovely. (*Works*, XIII, p. 416)

Having placed it in his Rudimentary Series, for teaching artists the basic skills of drawing, he was no doubt gratified that one amateur, the Revd W. Kingsley, copied the drawing nineteen times.

[1] A term used to describe students of mental disorders and early practitioners of psychiatry

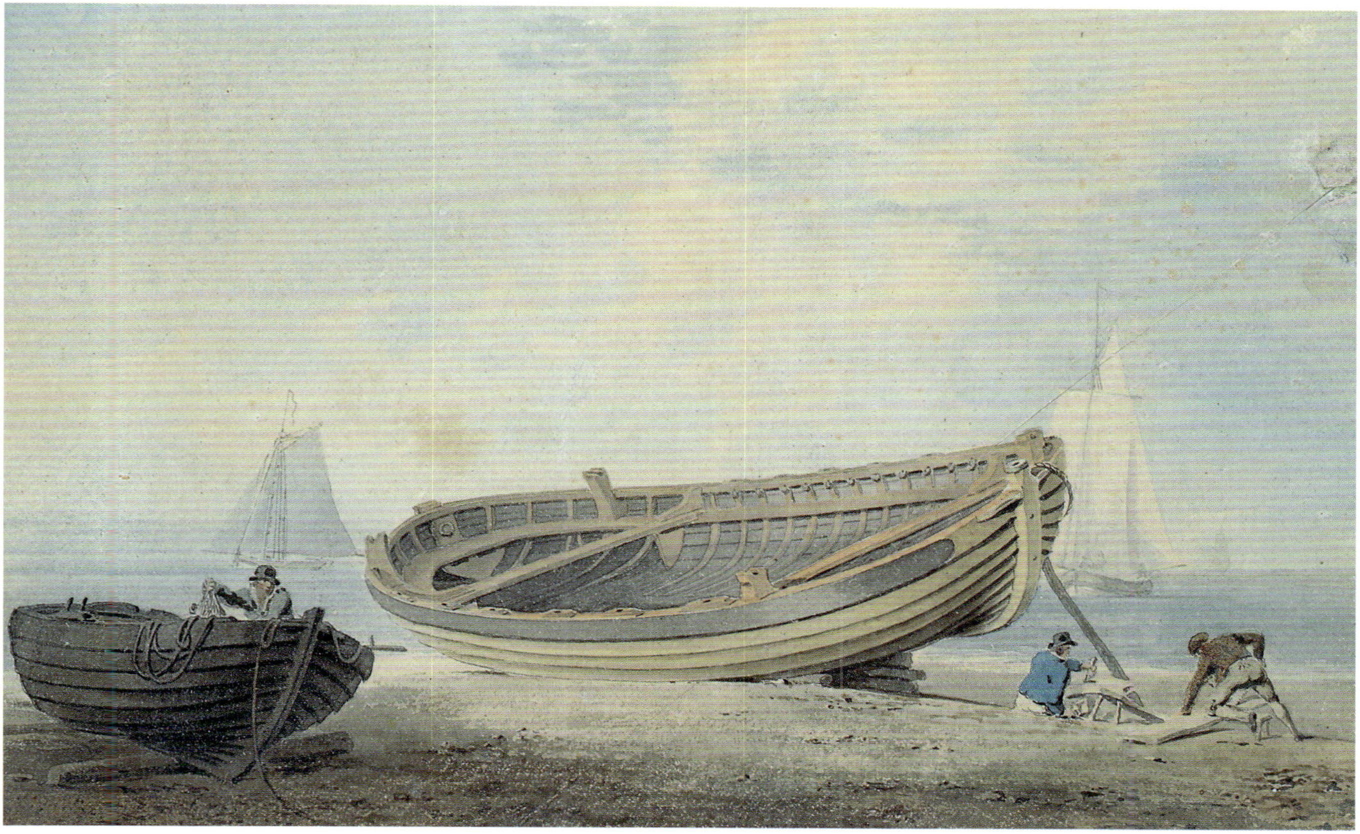

3 *'The Remains of Abingdon Abbey, now called Starve Castle'*

watercolours, with pen and black ink,
27 × 20.7 cm
inscribed in pen and ink, *The remains of Abingdon Abbey now called STARVE CASTLE ABINGDON* and signed, *Turner delin*
Bequeathed by A.E. Preston, F.S.A., 1942
[1942.14]
Herrmann 90; Wilton 39

From his uncle's home at Sunningwell, where he stayed after 1789, Turner must often have walked south to Abingdon and north up the Thames to Oxford. The abbey at Abingdon was an ancient Benedictine foundation dating from 670 and among the greatest in England until its dissolution by Henry VIII and subsequent demolition. Only the outbuildings survive, most prominently the magnificent chimney behind the Checker or treasury. Turner's watercolour is elaborately conceived and executed with extraordinary attention to detail. The view is taken looking south-east from Base Court towards the west. The sophisticated variety in the pen work, and masterly application of wash to evoke the sunlight on the brickwork, indicate a date of *c.*1793, and demonstrate the rapid progress Turner made in his youth. The waggon is included to draw attention to the modern function of the abbey, as a storehouse for grain, hence its name, Starve Castle, inscribed so boldly on the cart.

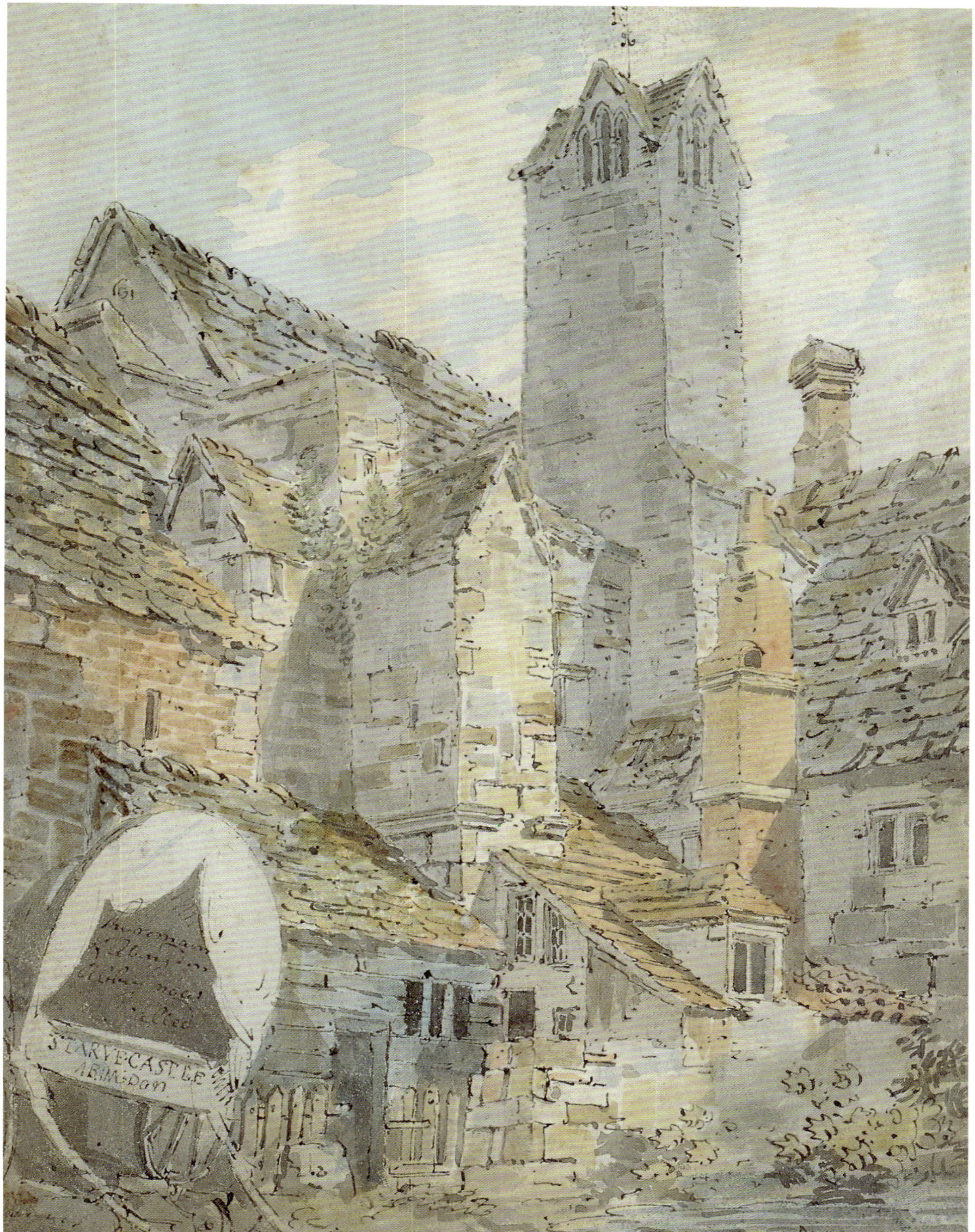
STARVECASTLE

4 *The Ruined Abbey at Haddington*

watercolours over pencil, 17.5 × 20.3 cm
Ruskin School Collection (Educational Series, no. 102)
Herrmann 60; Wilton 73

This unfinished watercolour is copied from an engraving by William Byrne after a watercolour by the antiquarian artist, Thomas Hearne, published in *The Antiquities of Great Britain* in 1786. It shows the river, town and bridge of Haddington, but Turner has enlarged the ruins and left the crossing in outline. The ruins had no doubt changed little by the time Turner first visited them in 1801. Turner copied another engraving of a Scottish subject after Hearne, of Edinburgh Castle, for John Henderson, in *c.*1794 (British Museum; Wilton 74), and *Haddington* may date from the same period.

Ruskin remarked of these copies, that,

> There are many drawings of this class in the National Gallery; few out of it; and of those few, it would be difficult to find one more perfectly demonstrative of the method of Turner's work. I can never get the public to believe, nor, until they believe it, can they ever understand, the grasp of a great master's mind, that, as in fresco, so in watercolour, there can be no retouching after your day's work is done; if you know what you want, you can do it at once, *then*; and if you don't, you cannot do it at all. There is absolute demonstration in this, and at least fifty other such unfinished pieces in the National Gallery, that Turner did his work bit by bit, finishing at once,and sure of his final harmony. When a given colour was needed over the whole picture, he would, of course, lay it over all at once and then go on with detail, over that, as he does here over white paper. I gave the drawing to the University Schools to be used in examination, a copy of it being required as a test of skill. (*Works*, XIII, pp. 415–6)

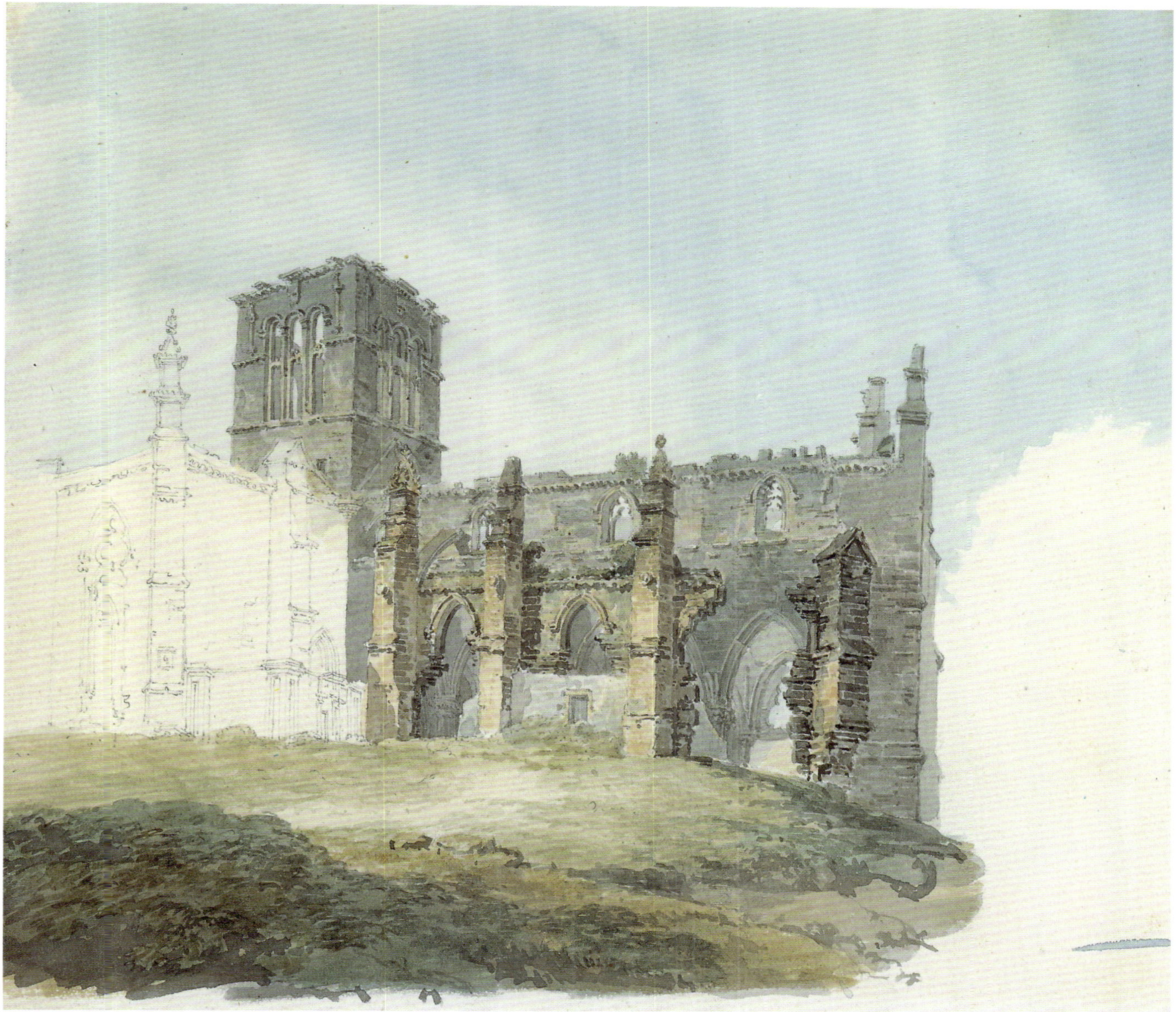

5 *'Transept of Tintern Abbey, Monmouthshire'*

pen and ink and watercolours over pencil,
35.5 × 26 cm
signed or inscribed in ink, *Turner*
Purchased (Magdalen College Fund), 1917
[1917.1]
Herrmann 91; Wilton 58

On his tour up the Wye in 1792, Turner must have spent several days at Tintern, for the pencil sketches provided him with the preparatory material for five watercolours, including the *Inside of Tintern Abbey, Monmouthshire* shown as Turner's first exhibit at the Royal Academy in 1794 (now in the Victoria and Albert Museum; Wilton 57). In the following year, he exhibited a different view, of the '*Transept of Tintern Abbey, Monmouthshire*', which was either no. 5 or a very similar work in the British Museum. Both are based on a large pencil drawing in outline, now at Wellesley College, Massachussets.

The watercolour in the Ashmolean was bought by the distinguished antiquary, amateur artist and patron of Girtin and Dayes, James Moore (1762–1799). He may have intended to publish it in his *Monastic Remains and Ancient Castles of England and Wales, drawn on the spot by James Moore*, which had begun to appear in 1792 but was never completed.

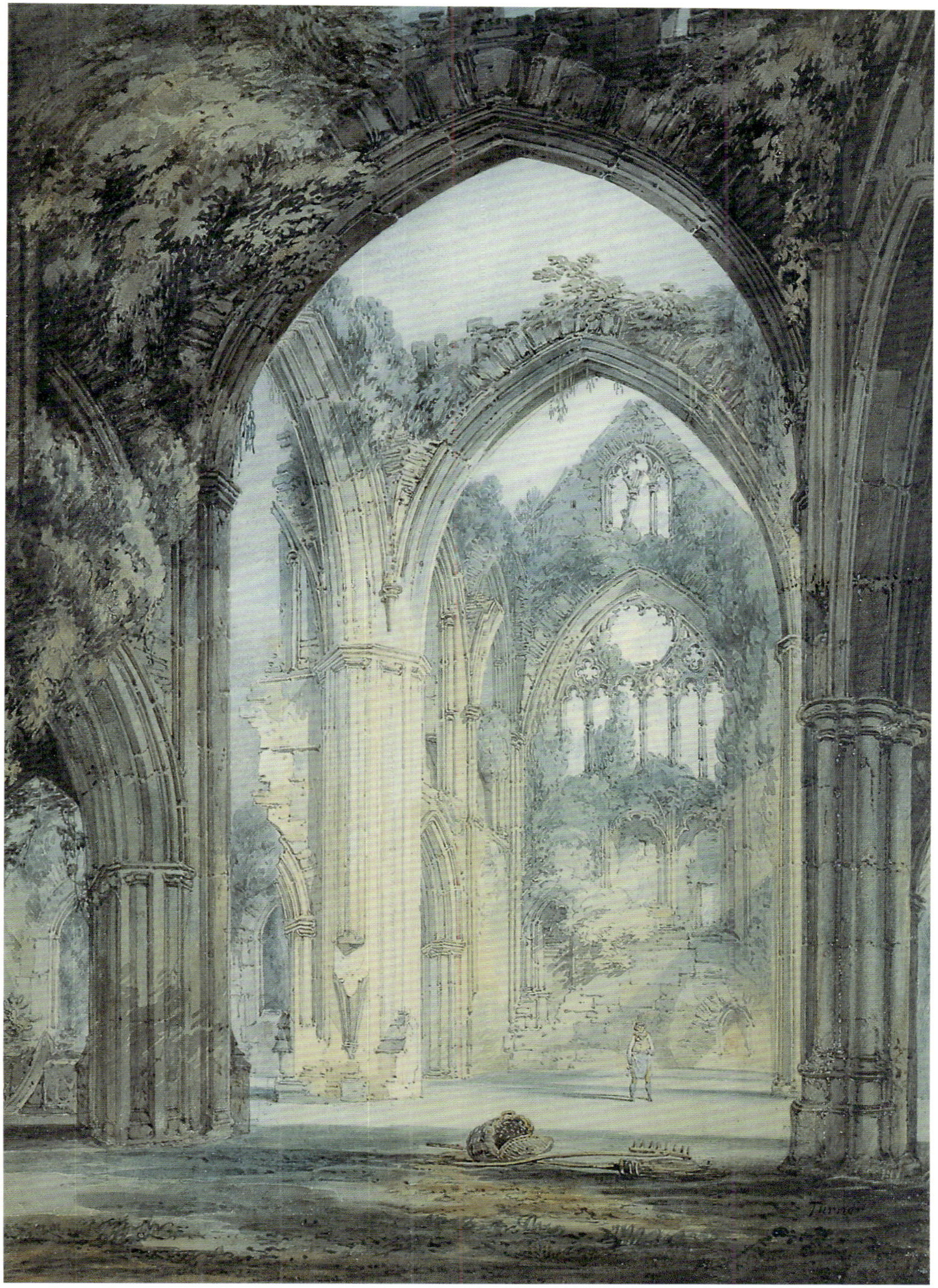
Turner

6 *Durham Castle from the River*

pencil, 36.6 × 26.3 cm
Ruskin School Collection (Educational Series, no. 126)
Herrmann 65

From an early age, Turner filled sketchbooks with summary and occasionally more elaborate drawings of subjects seen on his travels. Some 292 survive in the Tate Gallery, and dozens more can be reconstructed wholly or in part from dispersed sheets. This sketch of Durham is one such sheet, and comes from the so-called 'Tweed and Lakes' sketchbook, which included seven other views of Durham, as well as others in Yorkshire, Lancashire, and the Lake District. Turner used it in 1797, and, although this particular sketch was not used for a finished oil or watercolour, the silhouette of the castle appears in a watercolour of *Durham Cathedral from the River* made for the portrait painter, Joseph Hoppner, in the winter of 1798–9 (now in the Royal Academy; Wilton 249).

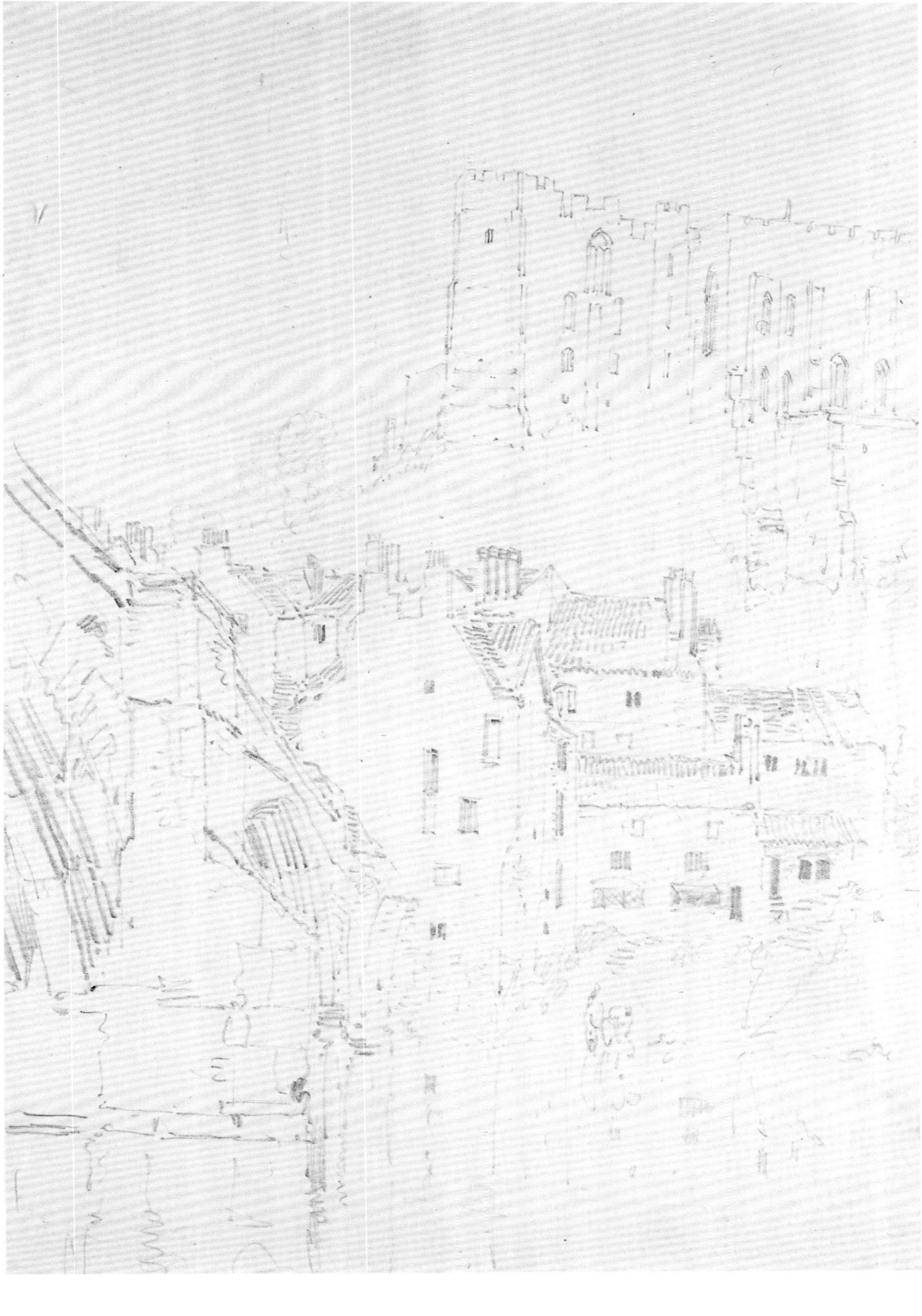

7 *'South View of Christ Church, &c. from the Meadows'*

watercolours, with some pen and black ink, over pencil, 31.5 × 45.1 cm
Deposited by the Delegates of the Clarendon Press, 1850 [1850.48]
Rawlinson 38; Herrmann 1; Petter, p. 81; Wilton 295

Christ Church, founded by Cardinal Wolsey in 1525, is the largest and, with its extensive meadows leading down to the stretch of the Thames known as the Isis, the most obviously picturesque college in Oxford, and it was therefore natural that Turner should have chosen it for his first drawing to be engraved as the headpiece for the Oxford Almanack. He obtained the commission for two initial designs in 1798–9, no doubt through his friend and master, Edward Dayes, who had supplied six drawings in 1794–5, not all of which had been engraved by 1799. Despite its apparent fading, this is one of Turner's most successful designs, translated, like all the engraved Almanacks, by the most skilful engravers of the time, James Basire, father and son.

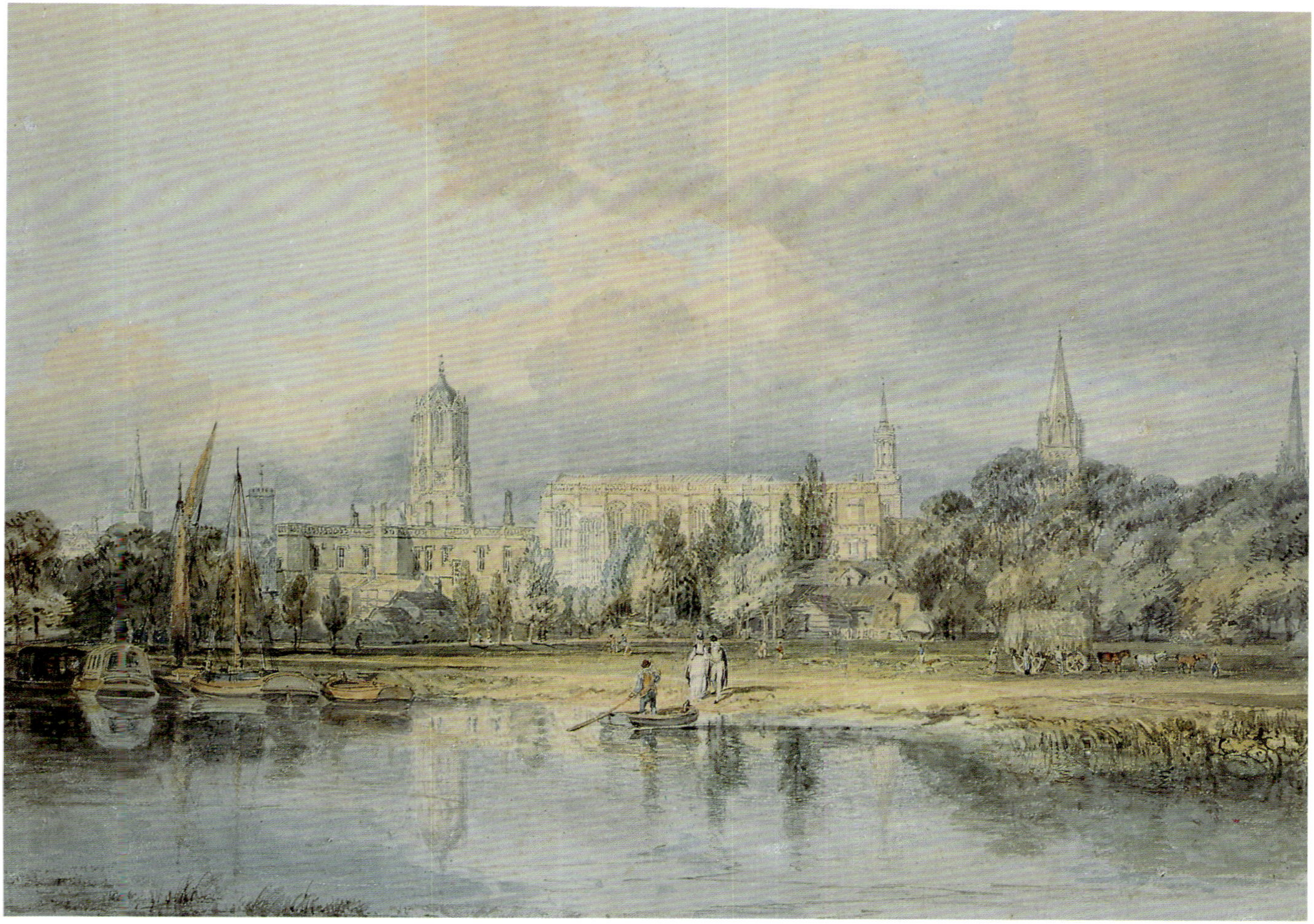

8 *'A View of Worcester College, &c.'*

watercolours over pencil, 32 × 44.3 cm
traces of signature, l.r.
Deposited by the Delegates of the Clarendon Press, 1850 [1850.52]
Rawlinson 41; Herrmann 4; Petter, pp. 82–3; Wilton 298

Following the success of the two watercolours commissioned for the Oxford Almanack in 1799, Turner made a further watercolour in 1801, and a group of seven in 1804, for which, despite his progress to full member of the Royal Academy in 1802, he was paid the same fee as before, i.e. ten guineas for each drawing. The view of Worcester was engraved by Basire for the Almanack of 1804. It shows the remarkably original entrance to the college, designed by Nicholas Hawksmoor and by Dr George Clarke of All Souls College, looking northwards past the surviving mediaeval buildings of the old Gloucester Hall, towards the Radcliffe Observatory, completed in 1794. Outside the college, figures repair the road that was later to become Beaumont Street, but are included as mere staffage rather than real workmen in 1804. The composition is carefully arranged so that the prominent Venetian windows on the wings of Worcester College dominate the foreground, and the road (now Walton Street) leads to the Observatory.

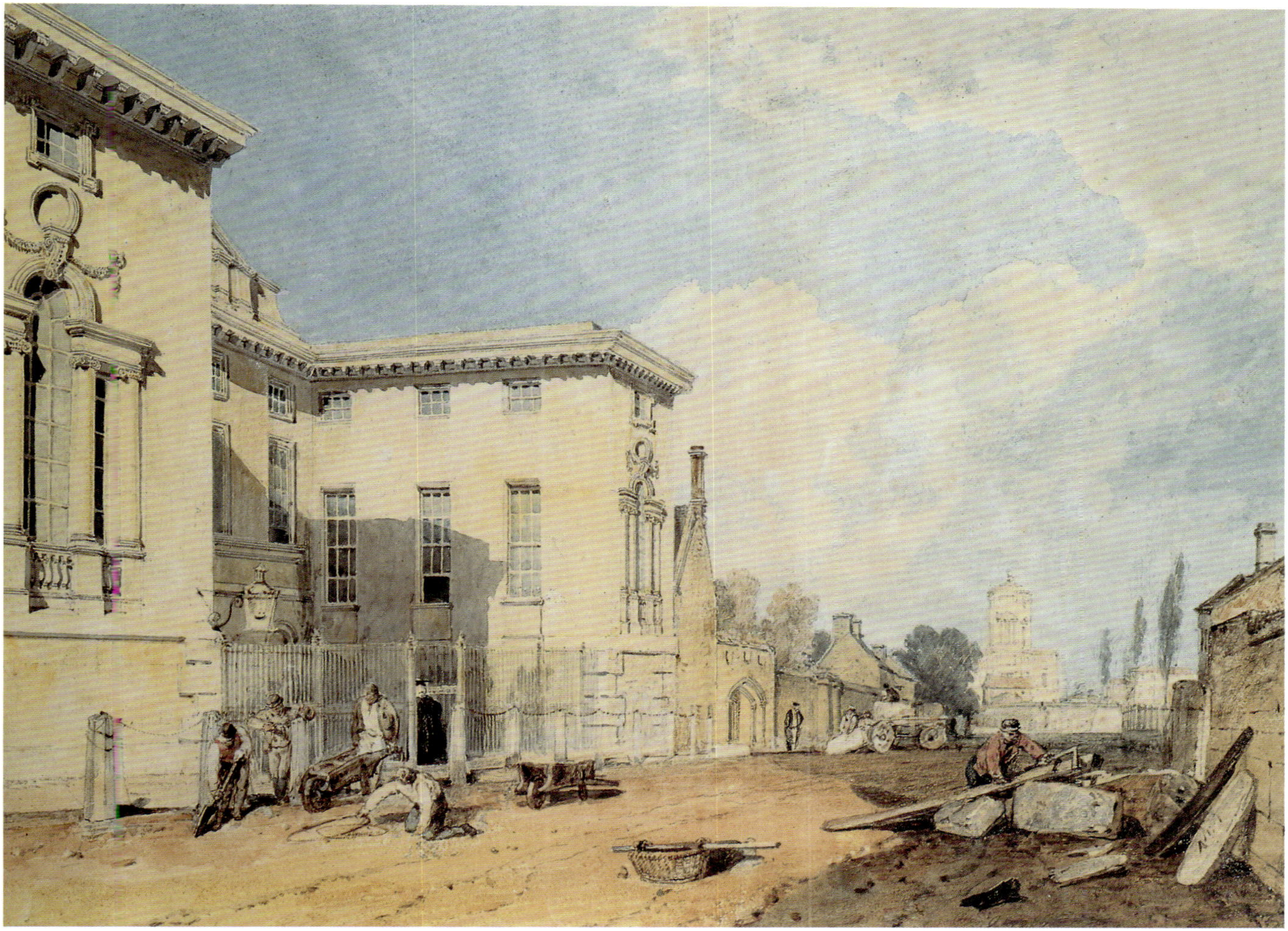

9 *View of Exeter College, All Saints Church &c. from the Turl*

brush in brown ink and watercolours over pencil, 32.1 × 45 cm
Deposited by the Delegates of the Clarendon Press, 1850 [1850.54]
Rawlinson 43; Herrmann 6; Petter, p. 83; Wilton 300

The design for the Oxford Almanack for 1806 shows Exeter College, erected during the great building boom in Oxford in the seventeenth century, with Jesus College opposite and Lincoln beyond, and the vista culminating in the distinctive spire of All Saints' Church on the High Street. The whole scene is lit by the afternoon sun of winter. As in the watercolour of Worcester, Turner has added road-menders as staffage, and manipulated the perspective to include all the picturesque elements. He has suggestively included two posters on the corner of the Turl and Ship Lane: one advertises a lecture at the Radcliffe Observatory; the other, a performance at the theatre. The original sketch for the watercolour must have included the hatchment over the gate of Jesus College, indicating that it was drawn shortly after the death of the Principal, Dr Joseph Hoare, in 1802; this incidental detail is included in the watercolour but not the engraving.

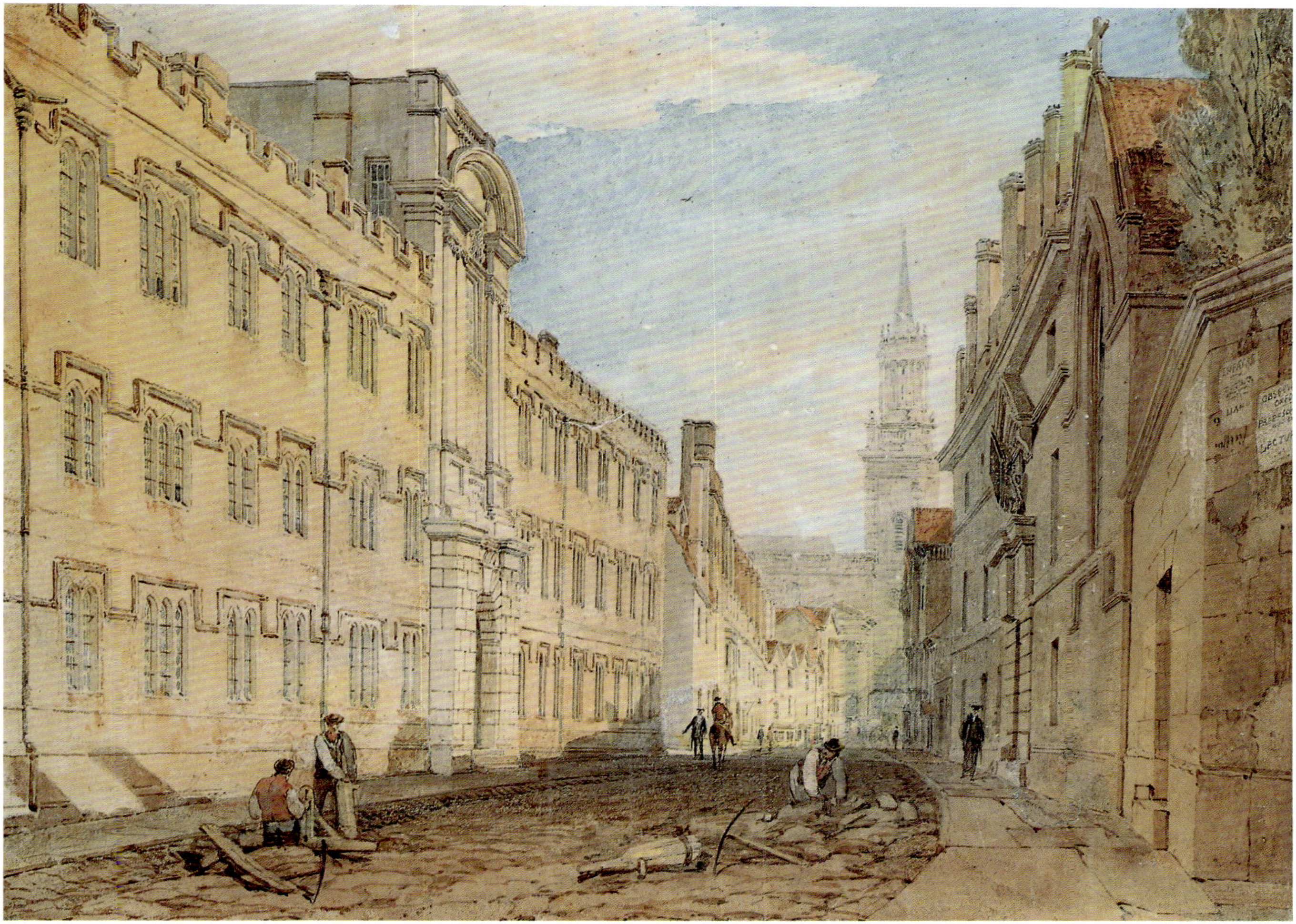

10 *Inside View of the Hall of Christ Church*

watercolours over pencil, with scratching out, 32.9 × 44.8 cm
Deposited by the Delegates of the Clarendon Press, 1850 [1850.55]
Rawlinson 44; Herrmann 7; Petter, pp. 83–4; Wilton 301

The Delegates of the Clarendon Press were apparently delighted with Turner's first six designs for the Almanack, but in 1806, they gave instructions that 'Mr. Neill be commissioned to sketch more correctly some parts of the inside of Christ Church Hall, for the use of the Engraver of the Almanack for the ensuing year.' Hugh O'Neill (1784–1824), who was eventually to replace Turner as the draughtsman for the Almanack, was a pedestrian local artist, whose enthusiasm for accuracy matched Turner's for poetry. The nature of his revisions of the view of Christ Church hall is not known, but comparison between the drawing and the engraving reveals only slight differences, mostly in the larger size and greater distinctiveness of the portraits. One unusual aspect of Turner's drawing is the amount of scratching out of the pigment to reveal the white paper as highlights below, especially in the gilt picture frames and the roof. Highly effective as it is, this may have been done on the instructions of the Delegates.

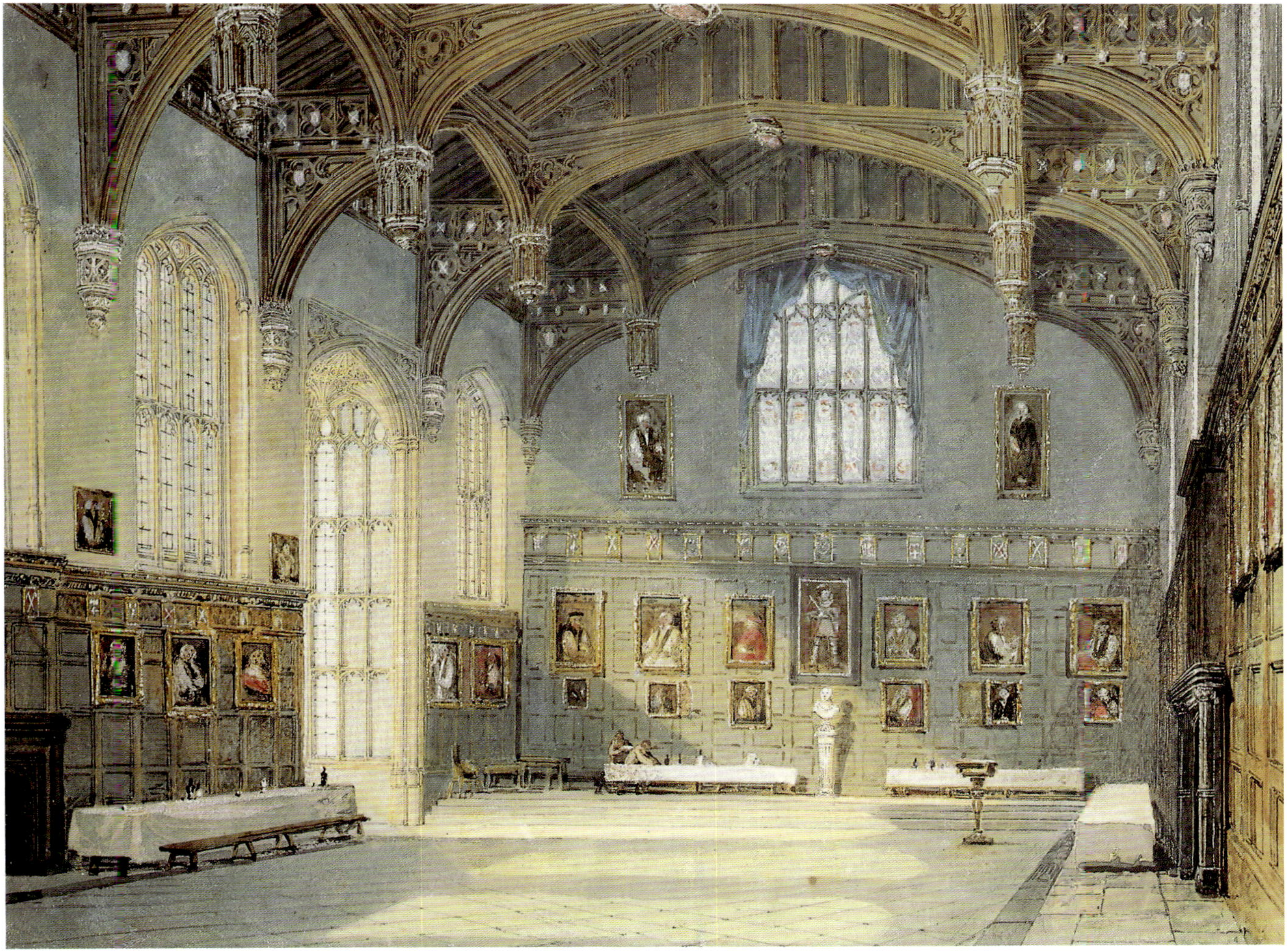

11 *Lake of Thun*

etching, drypoint and mezzotint, 18.2 × 26.4 cm (plate)
inscr. *M Drawn & Etchd by J.M.W. Turner Esqr. R.A.P.P. / Engraved by C.Turner. // LAKE OF THUN, SWISS / London Published June 10. 1808 by C.Turner, No. 50 Warren Street Fitzroy Square*
Ruskin School Collection
Finberg 15, state ii

The *Liber Studiorum* was a series of prints after drawings by Turner which the artist himself controlled, usually making the preliminary etching himself. 71 prints of the projected 100 were published in fourteen parts between 1807 and 1819, with a further 20 plates more or less completed but never published. In the prospectus, Turner wrote that 'it is intended in this publication to attempt a description of the various styles of landscape, viz., the historic, mountainous, pastoral, marine, and architectural', indicated on each plate by the initials H, M, P, M, and A. He later added a sixth category, EP, which may stand for 'Elevated Pastoral', and which became one of the most numerous.

This dramatic subject was derived from a sketch made on the tour of Switzerland in 1802, which Turner developed in a larger watercolour a few years later. The engraving by Charles Turner, in the 'mountainous' category, was published in part 3 of the *Liber Studiorum*.

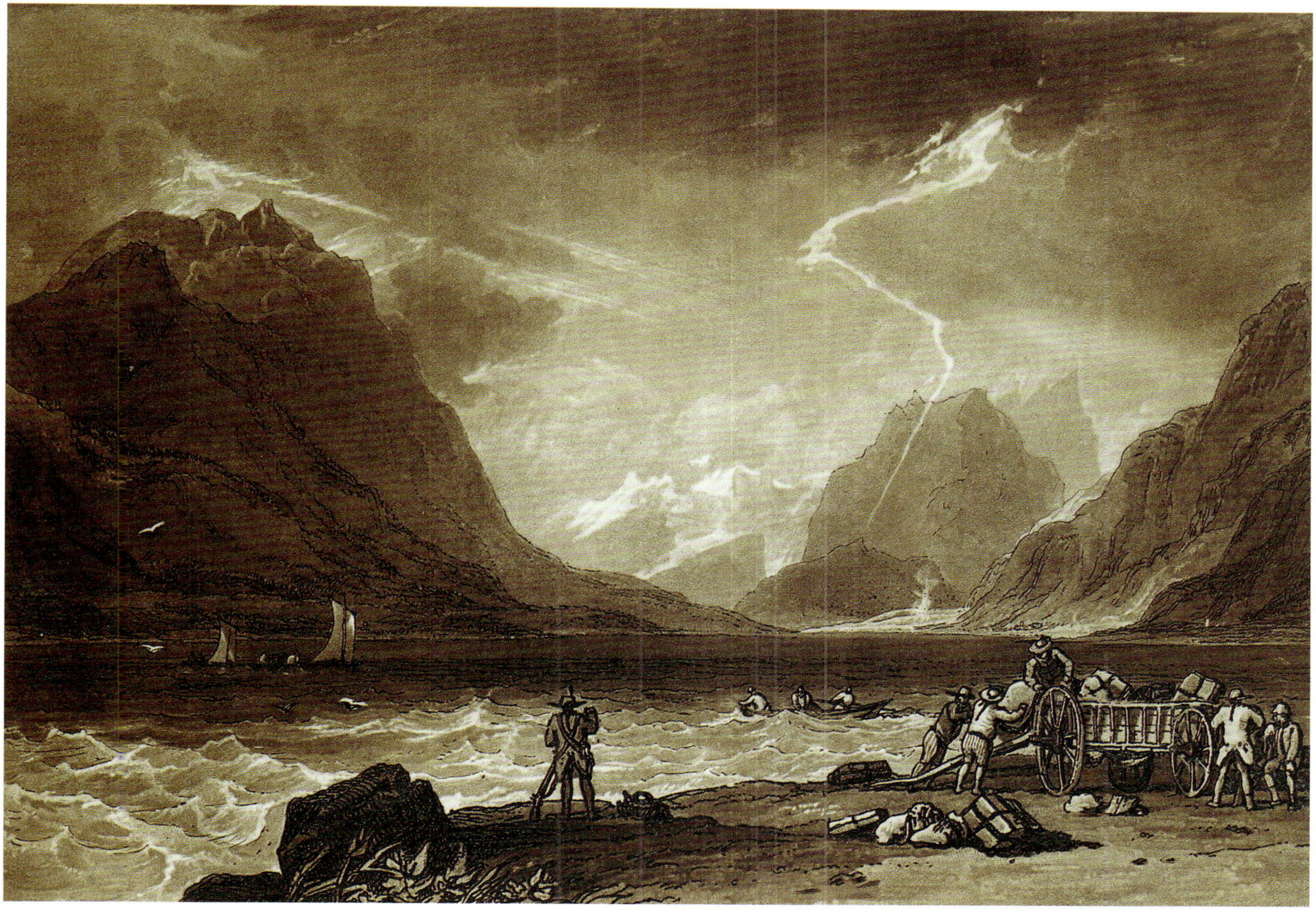

12 *Study of a Group of Cows*

watercolours over pencil with scratching out, 21.6 × 32.4 cm
Ruskin School Collection (Educational Series, no. 185)
Herrmann 71; Wilton 409

Apart from the watercolours of birds and fishes made at Farnley in 1815, Turner made few studies of animals. This drawing, described by Ruskin as 'quite insuperable in perfection of rapid sketching,' may be related to pencil sketches in the 'Cow' sketchbook of 1801 (T.B. LXII). Such studies provided the basis for the groups of cows in the pastoral idylls in oils, such as the following picture.

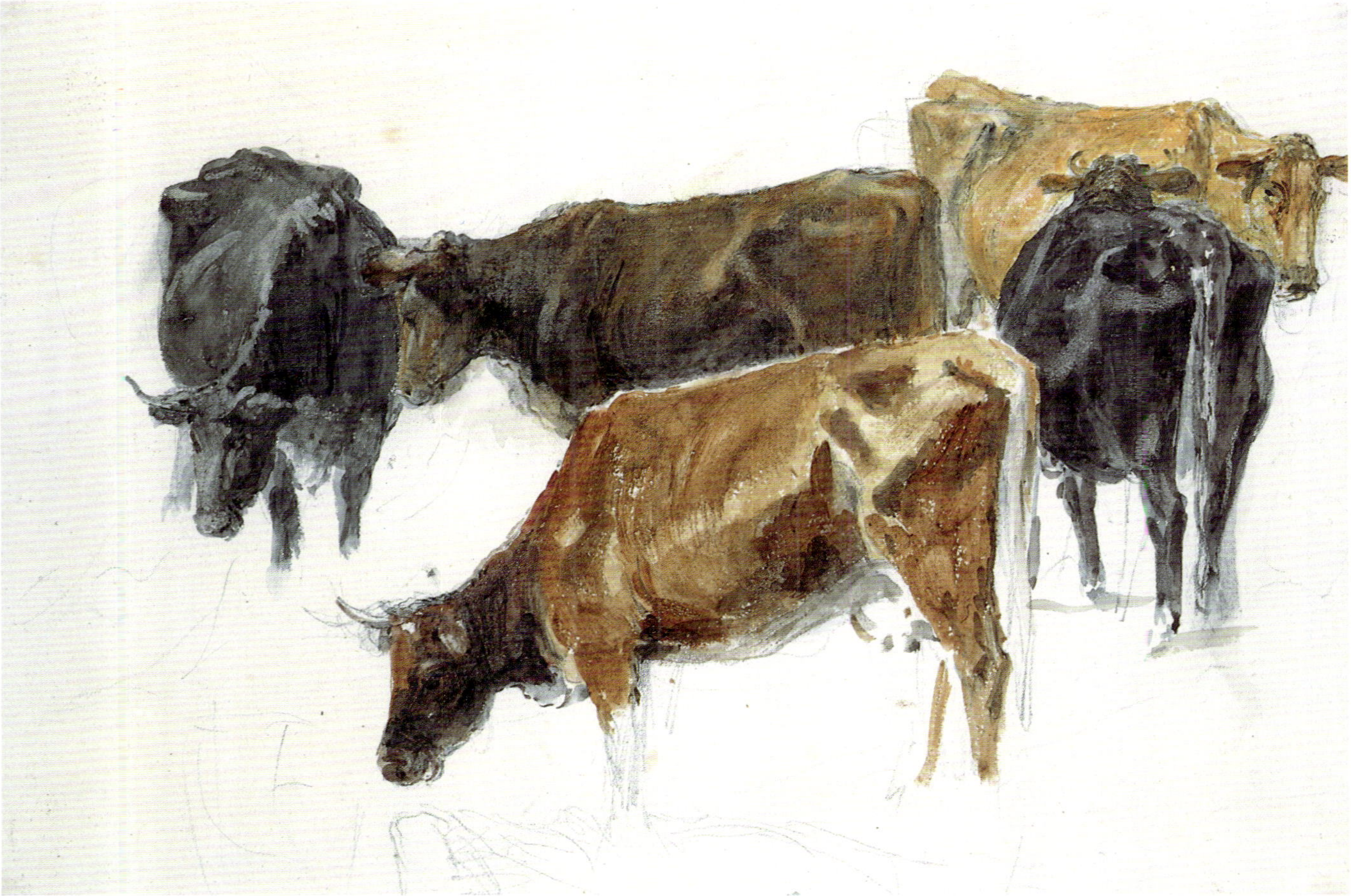

oil on canvas, 92.7 × 123.8 cm
signed, lower right, *JMW Turner RA*
Prov.: Sir John Leicester; Thomas Wright of Upton; Joseph Gillot; H.W.F. Bolckow; Lord Wantage, and by descent
Lent from the Loyd Collection (L.97.140)
Butlin & Joll 60

The picturesque bridges over the Thames at Walton were great favourites with artists: the old wooden structure was painted several times by Canaletto, and the new twin stone bridges twice by Turner in 1806–7 and again in the 1840s. Both the earlier paintings (the other is in the National Gallery of Victoria, Melbourne) were based on studies made on a tour of the Thames in 1805. Here, Turner has transformed these topographical beginnings into a spacious and airy pastoral idyll bathed in warm evening light, with cows watering and men mooring their boats for the night.

This painting was probably exhibited at Turner's gallery in 1806; it was certainly bought for £280 by Sir John Leicester in January 1807. Sir John, of Tabley Hall, Cheshire, had been forming a collection of modern British paintings at his London residence at 24 Hill Street, Mayfair, which he intended should be bought by the nation as the basis of a National Gallery of British Art. Among other works, he owned a further nine by Turner, among them *The Falls of the Rhine at Schaffhausen* (Butlin & Joll 61), and two views of Tabley, completed in 1809 (Butlin & Joll 98–9). However, Leicester seems to have tried to sell *Walton Bridges* soon after he bought it, and it never occupied its rightful place in his galleries.

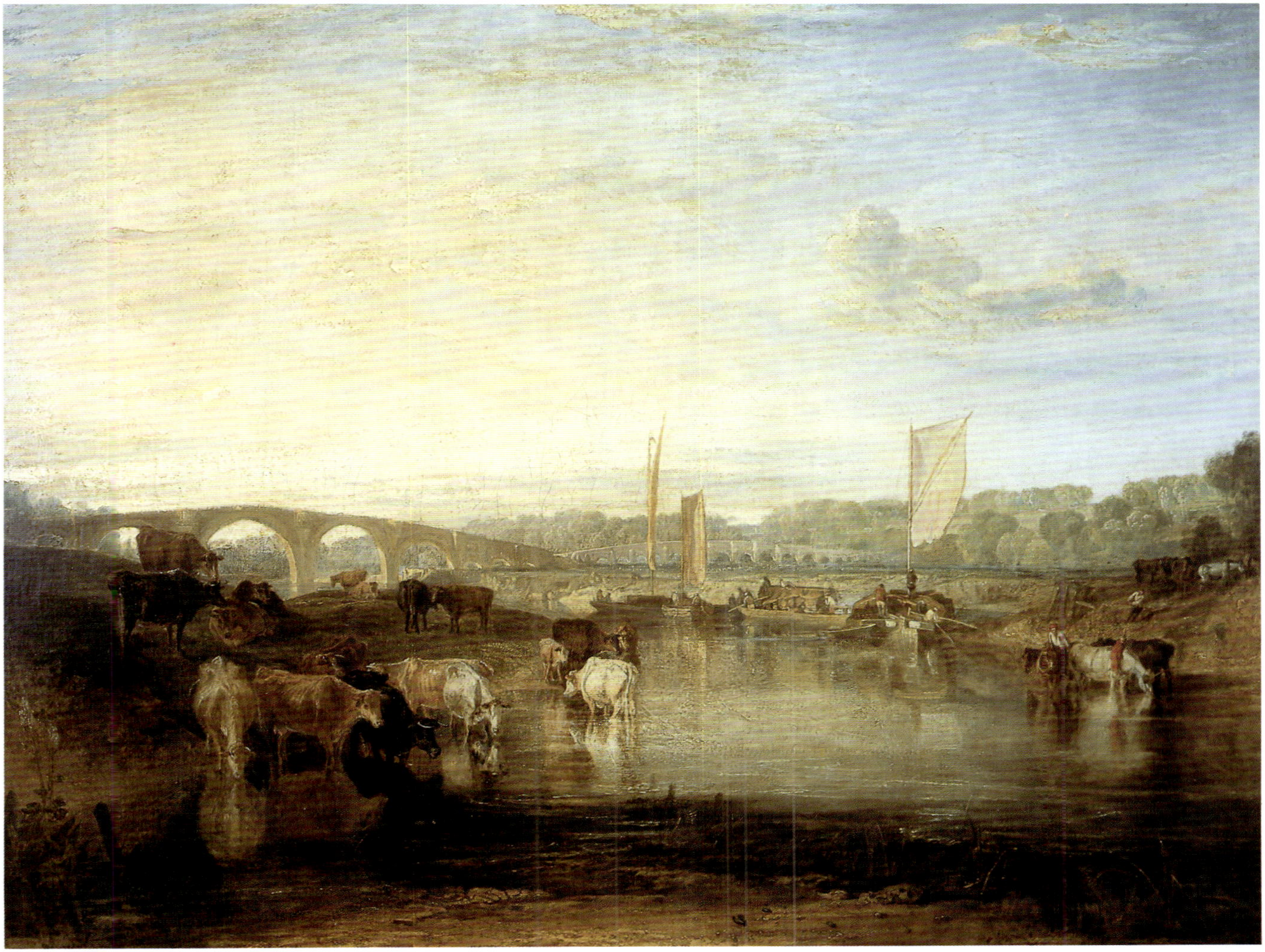

14 *Park Scene: Distant View of Lowther Castle*

watercolours and pencil, 22.4 × 35.2 cm
Prov.: Revd W. Kingsley; John Ruskin
Ruskin School Collection (Educational Series, no. 128)
Herrmann 72; Wilton 524

Another of Turner's patrons during his middle period was William, first Earl of Lonsdale (1757–1844), who, following the success of the two views of Tabley in 1809, commissioned two views of his own seat, Lowther Castle in Westmorland, which were exhibited at the Royal Academy in 1810 (Butlin & Joll 111–2). They were based on preliminary sketches made in the summer of 1809, of which three are in the Ashmolean. Passages from the present sketch were incorporated into both paintings: the general appearance is similar to the view at *Mid-Day*, while the thistle in the foreground appears in the view at *Evening*. This is the only sketch to be partially reworked in watercolours, suggesting that Turner decided while working on it that the pencil sketches were sufficient for his needs.

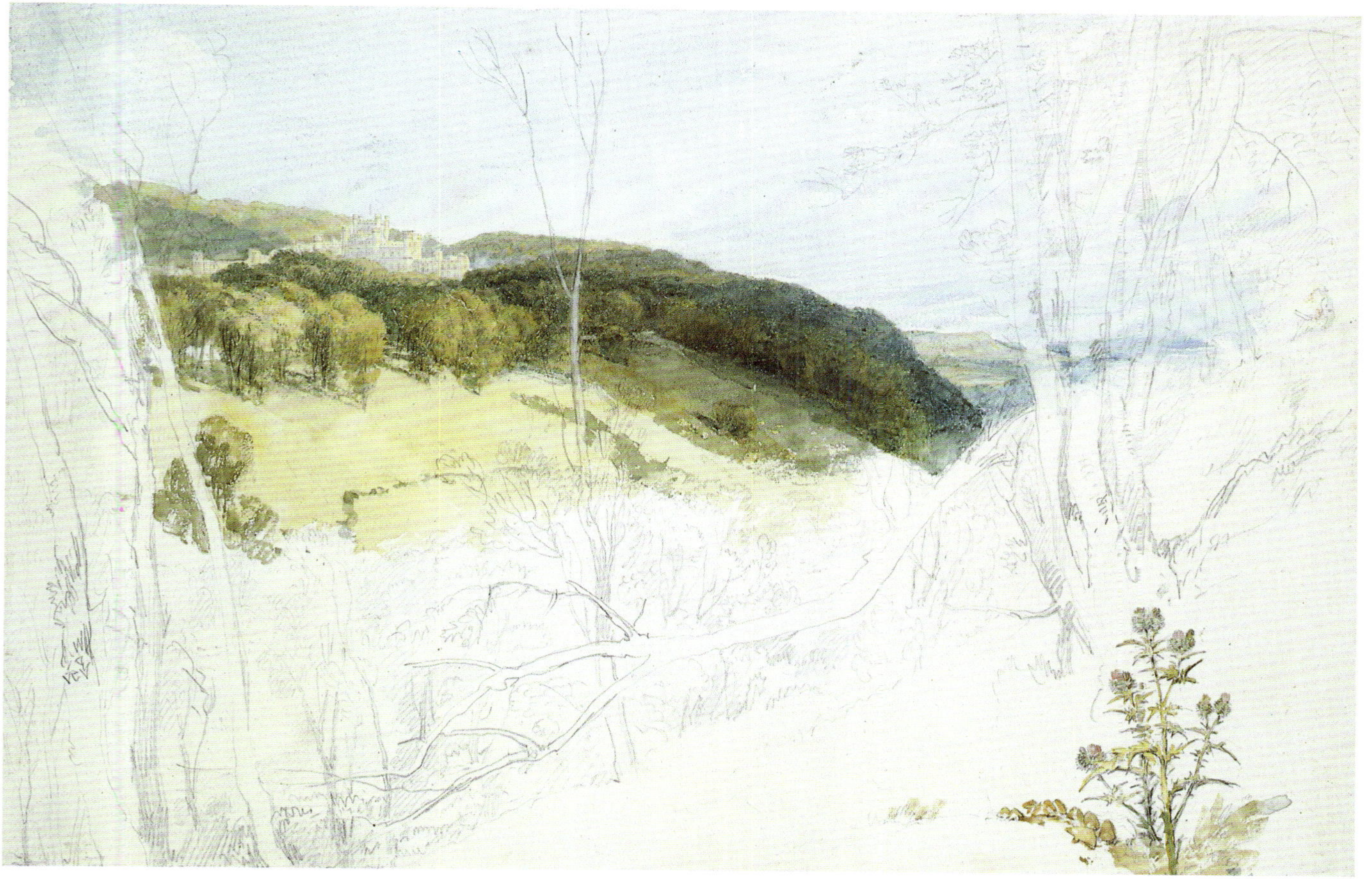

15 *High Street, Oxford*

oil on canvas, 68.5 × 100.3 cm
signed, lower right, *IMW Turner RA*
Prov.: James Wyatt; Mrs Jesse Watts Russell; Lord Overstone, and by descent
Lent from the Loyd Collection (L.97.141)
Butlin & Joll 102

James Wyatt (1774–1853), who dealt in pictures, frames, and prints at 115 High Street, Oxford, decided in 1809 to commission a work from Turner in order to sell engravings after it. Initially, he hesitated between a watercolour and an oil painting, and settled on an oil rather smaller than Turner's norm, for which he would pay 100 guineas. The extensive surviving correspondence[1] suggests that Turner was more than usually keen to please, consulting Wyatt on such details as the number, character and costumes of the figures, and the precise drawing of architectural details. It was, however, Turner who decided to add two female figures 'for the sake of colour'. He made the initial sketch in December 1809, and delivered the finished painting in April, 1810. Wyatt was delighted, and not only paid Turner the agreed fee, but also sent him a gift of game and sausages. More materially, he commissioned a pendant, *Oxford from the Abingdon Road* (private collection; Butlin and Joll 125), and allowed both paintings to be exhibited at the Royal Academy in 1812, where they were hung so high as to be invisible.

The engraving, by the best engravers of Turner's middle years, Pye and Middiman, with the figures by Charles Heath, is dated 14 March 1812, but was in fact completed shortly afterwards, while that of the companion painting was not published until 1818 (Rawlinson 80).

[1] *Correspondence*, ed. Gage, pp. 38–42, 52

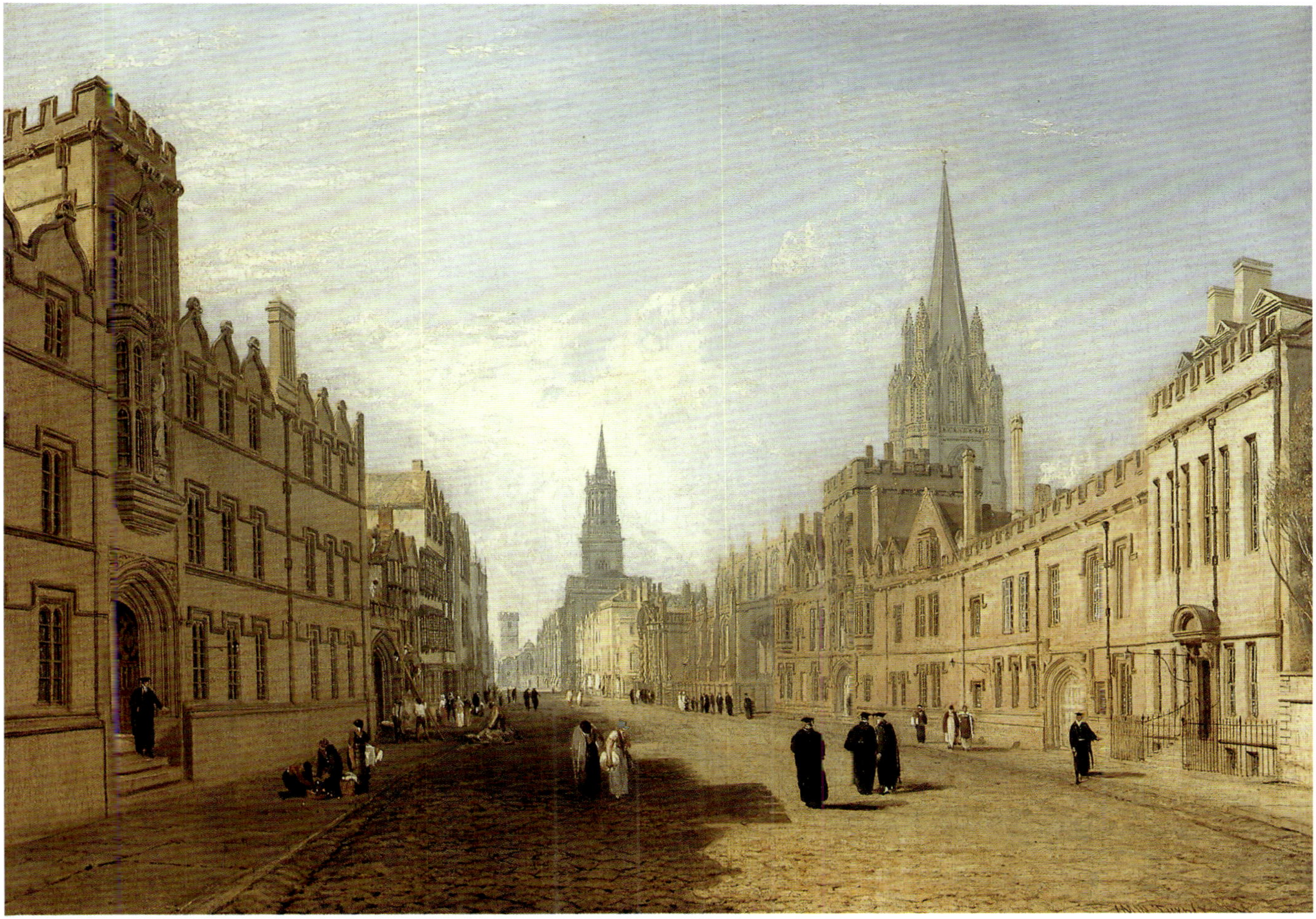

16 *Whalley Bridge and Abbey, Lancashire: Dyers washing and drying Cloth*

oil on canvas, 61.2 × 92 cm
Prov.: Thomas Lister Parker; J. Newington Hughes; Wynn Ellis; Lord Overstone, and by descent
Lent from the Loyd Collection (L.97.142)
Butlin & Joll 117

This composition is based on a sketch made in 1808, when Turner was visiting Sir John Leicester. The oil may have been commissioned by Sir John's neighbour, Thomas Lister Parker, who had collaborated with Whitaker on the *History of Whalley* (1800–1). It was one of the first paintings Turner made on a white ground, and is a notable example of Turner's ability to imbue the English countryside with a mood of Claudean elegy.

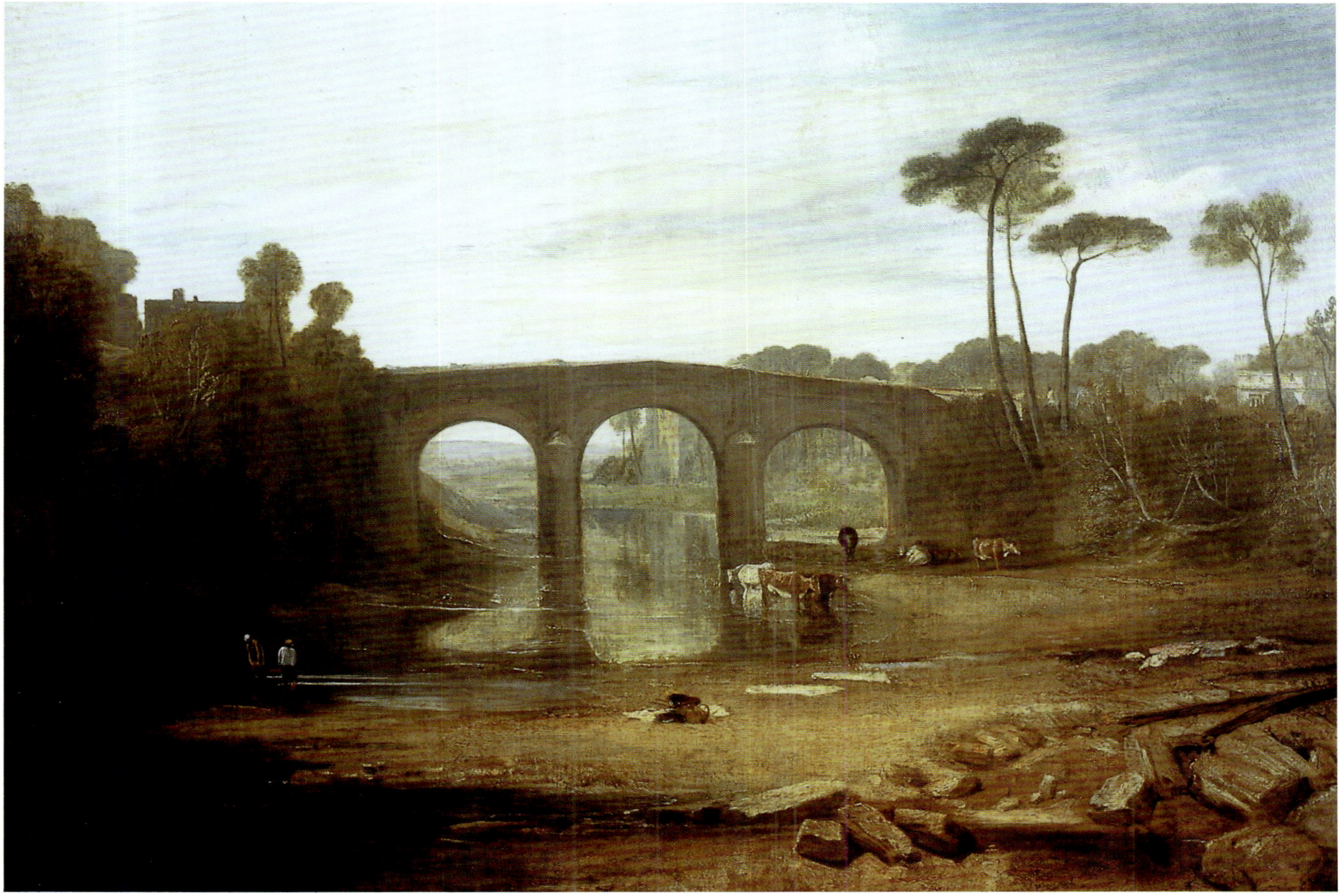

17 *Study of Trees*

pen and brown ink and wash over pencil,
22.6 × 33.6 cm
Ruskin School Collection (Rudimentary Series, no. 300)
Herrmann 75

Ruskin 'prized this drawing' as one of his 'very chief Turner treasures' (*Works*, XXI, p. 298), long believing it to be a study for one of the unpublished plates in the *Liber Studiorum*. More recently, it has been suggested that it is related to a very early trial proof from an unfinished plate for the *Liber* (Forrester, p.21). In any case, the technique is comparable with that of preparatory drawings for this project, dating from *c.*1812–15. A close parallel is the study for *Berry Pomeroy Castle*, of which this may be an alternative version (Finberg 58).

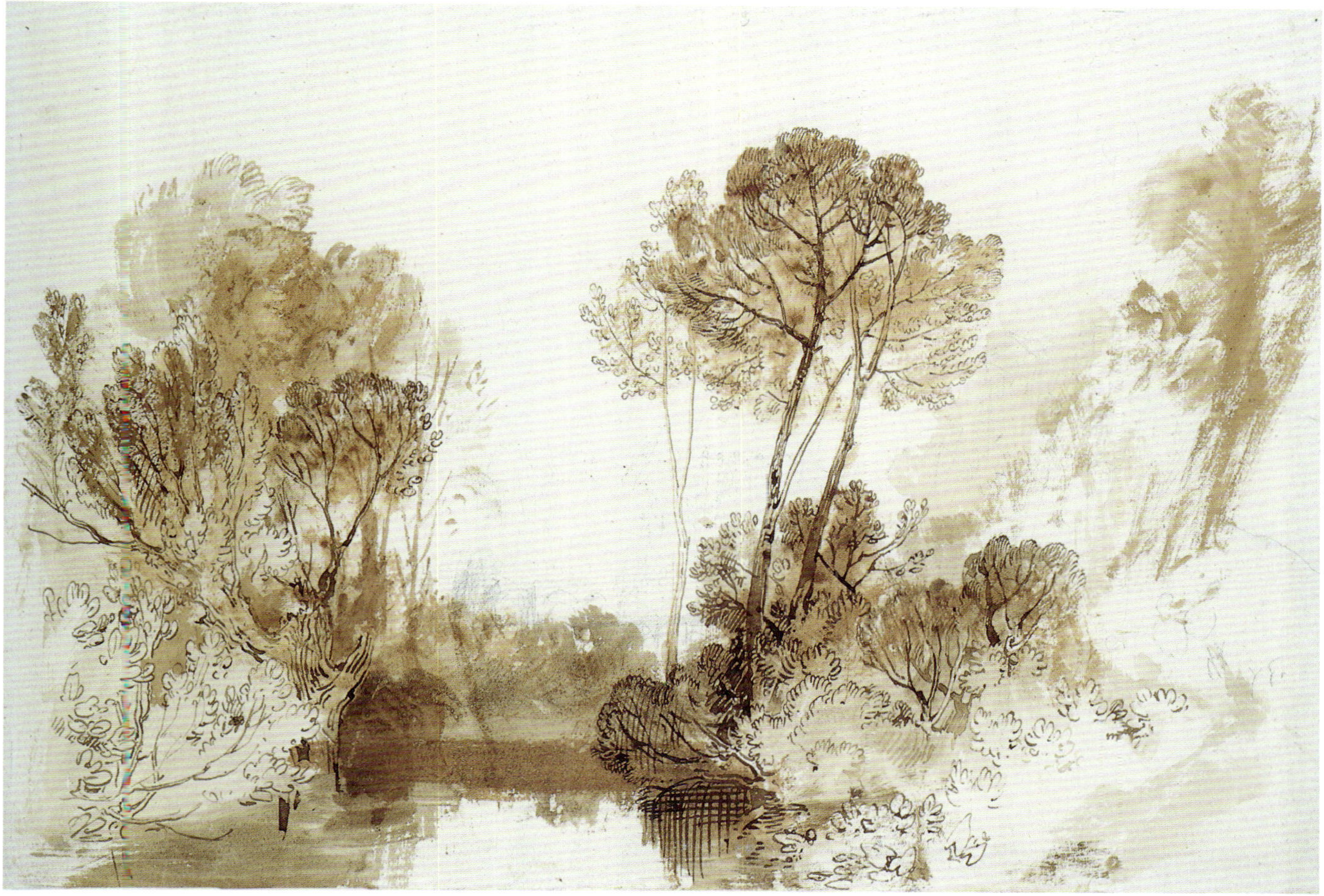

18 *Sunshine on the Tamar*

watercolours with some scratching out, 21.7 × 36.7 cm
Ruskin School Collection (Reference Series, no. 168)
Herrmann 76; Wilton 444

The precise site of this drawing has eluded identification: both the River Tamar and the Tavey flow into the sea at Plymouth, and Turner made the preliminary sketch for this watercolour during a tour of Devonshire in 1813. The watercolour was no doubt made in connexion with the projected volume of *The Rivers of Devon*, which W.B. Cooke planned at the same time as the *Picturesque Views on the Southern Coast of England* (see no. 23). Only four watercolours were engraved (Rawlinson 137–40), while this, the most poetic, was not.

This drawing, 'small as it is', cost Ruskin 650 guineas, and he was evidently much taken with it, initially christening it *Pigs in Sunshine; Scene on the Tavey, Devonshire*, and later referring to it as *Pigs by Sunlight*. Although he later gave it the present, more decororous, title, the pigs still preoccupied him when he described the drawing in 1878 as showing 'already one of Turner's specially English (in the humiliating sense) points of character – that, like Bewick, he could draw *pigs* better than any other animal. There is also some trace of Turner's constant feeling afterwards. Sunshine, and rivers, and sweet hills; yes, and who is there to see or care for them? – Only the pigs.' (*Works*, XIII, pp. 433–5)

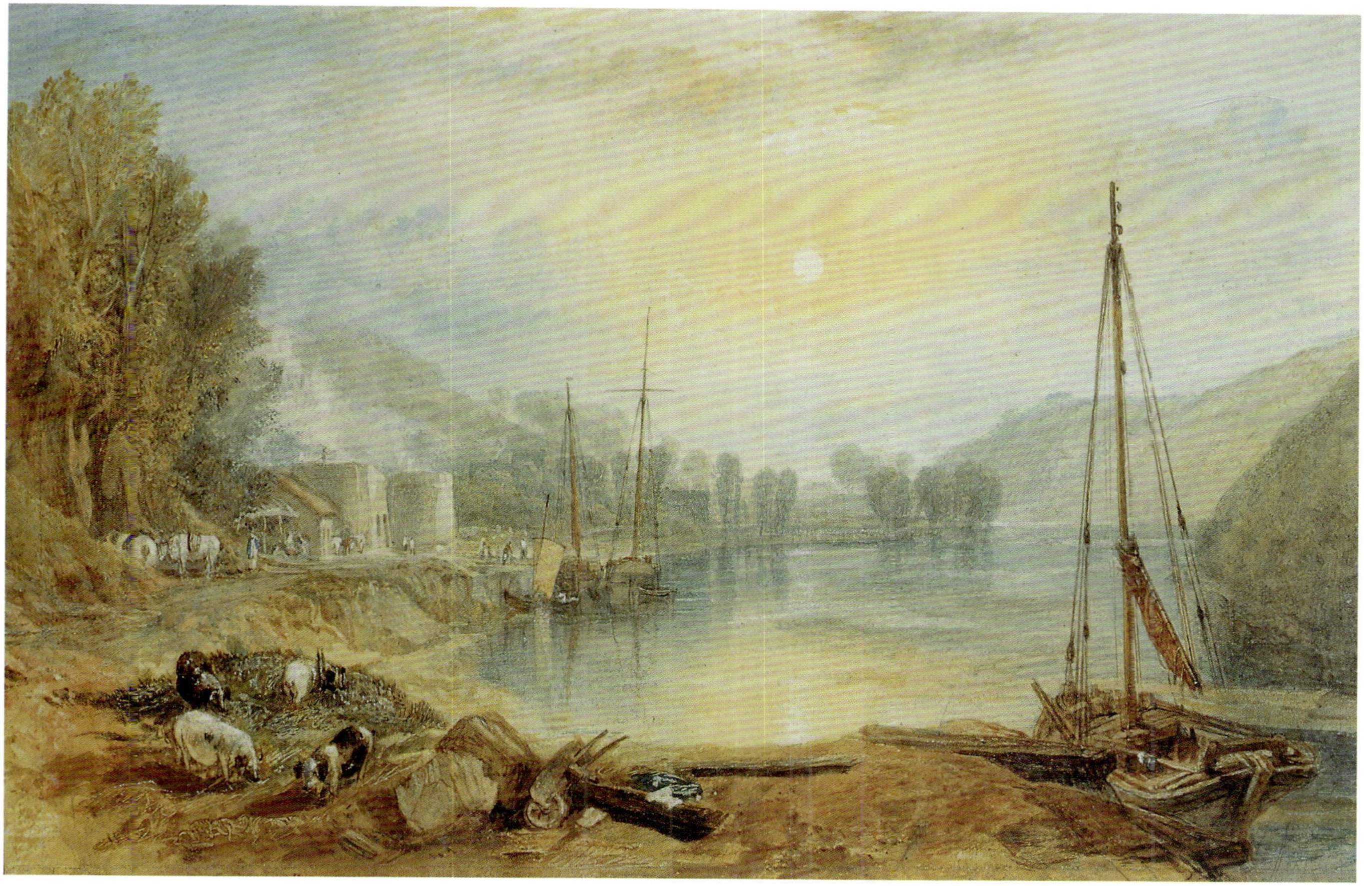

19 *A Frontispiece (at Farnley Hall)*

watercolours over pencil, with pen and ink and scratching out, 17.8 × 24.2 cm
signed and dated in ink, lower left: *J.M.W. Turner RA 1815*
Prov.: Walter Fawkes; Charles Stokes; Ruskin
Ruskin School Collection (Rudimentary Series, no. 14)
Herrmann 77; Wilton 582

Walter Fawkes, squire of Farnley Hall near Leeds, was one of Turner's closest friends and his greatest patron, eventually owning over 200 watercolours and six oil paintings. At Farnley, Turner enjoyed conversation, antiquarianism, and shooting, and his work reflected his interests. Ruskin acquired this drawing in exchange for some *Liber* proofs from his stockbroker, Charles Stokes, who told him that

> 'Fairfaxiana', said the artist, 'are a set of drawings I made for Mr Fawkes of subjects relating to the Fairfax property which came into Mr Fawkes' family, and I did this for the frontispiece. The helmet, drinking-cup, and sword were those of a knight of that family who was called Black Jack. The *Illustrated London News* got hold of it, and copied the helmet and sword.'

There were apparently some fifteen watercolours in the set, the remainder views of the exterior and interior of Farnley Hall.

In 1878, Ruskin wrote,

> Examine with lens the beautifully legible signature of Oliver Cromwell on the smallest of the fallen papers; also under the helmet the writing of the pedigree of the Farnley family. As brush-work, the sentence "they are sometimes", and the perfectly free "Hawkesworth" and "Richmond" will give a general idea of the ease of Turner's hand in minute lines. The colour of the shields on the principal scroll, and the lion rampant on the standard of Fairfax are to be copied by all students as soon as they have attained some facility in watercolour. The lion being executed with a wash of grey over the underlying vermilion bars, and the roughnesses given by only one process of retouching, with a scratch or two of the knife to conquer the vermilion, is of extremist value as a watercolour exercise. The drawing once belonged to Mr Fawkes of Farnley, and had been frightfully injured by ill-usage on the left-hand side of it before it came into my possession. (*Works*, XXI, pp. 174–5)

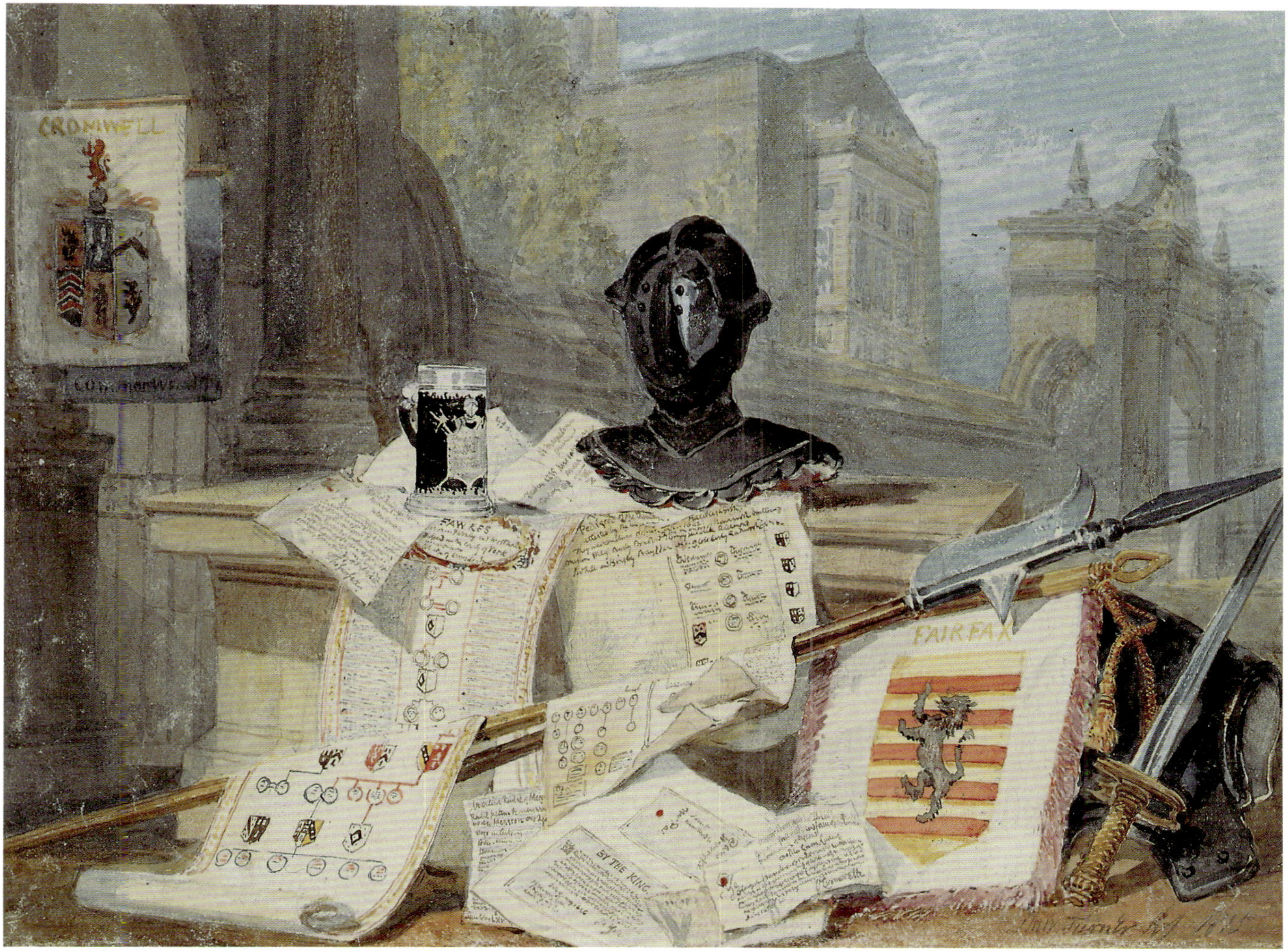
CROMWELL
FAWKES
FAIRFAX
BY THE KING

20 *The Junction of the Greta and Tees at Rokeby*

watercolours over pencil, with scratching out,
29 × 41.4 cm
Prov.: J. Dillon; Ruskin
Ruskin School Collection (Standard Series, no. 2)
Herrmann 79; Wilton 566

This grand and atmospheric watercolour was based on a sketch made while Turner was touring in Yorkshire in 1816. It was one of a group of watercolours made in 1817–18 for Whitaker's *History of Richmondshire*, and was engraved on copper by John Pye (Rawlinson 175).

Ruskin believed this watercolour, which had cost him 500 guineas, to be his best example of Turner's work, describing it as

> a faultless example of Turner's work at the time when it is most exemplary. It will serve us for various illustrations as we advance in the study of landscape, but it may be well to note of it at once, that in the painting of the light falling on the surface of the Tees, and shining through the thicket above the Greta, it is an unrivalled example of chiaroscuro of the most subtle kind; obtained by the slightest possible contrasts, and by consummate skill in the management of gradation. The rock and stone drawing is not less wonderful, and entirely good as a lesson in practice. (*Works*, XXI, pp. 169–70)

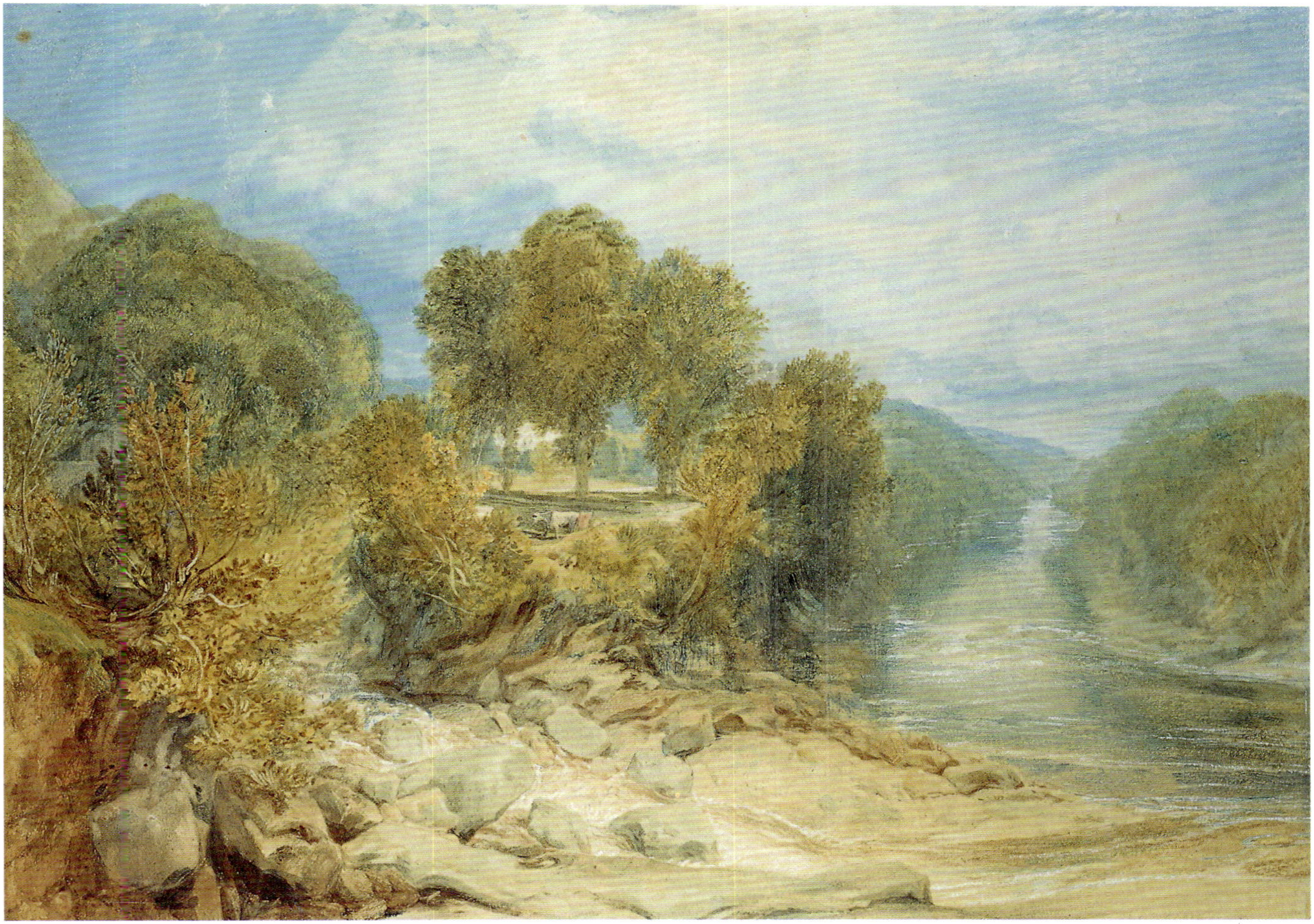

21 *Study of a Mackerel*

watercolours over pencil, 22.4 × 28.7 cm
Ruskin School Collection (Educational Series, no. 182)
Herrmann 80; Wilton 1399

Ruskin owned two other sketches of mackerel, which he noted were

> all executed with a view mainly to colour, and, in colour, to its ultimate refinements, as in the grey down of the birds and the subdued iridescences of the fish. There is no execution in watercolour comparable to them for combining rapidity, delicacy and precision – the artists of the world may be challenged to approach them.
> (*Works*, XIII, p. 370)

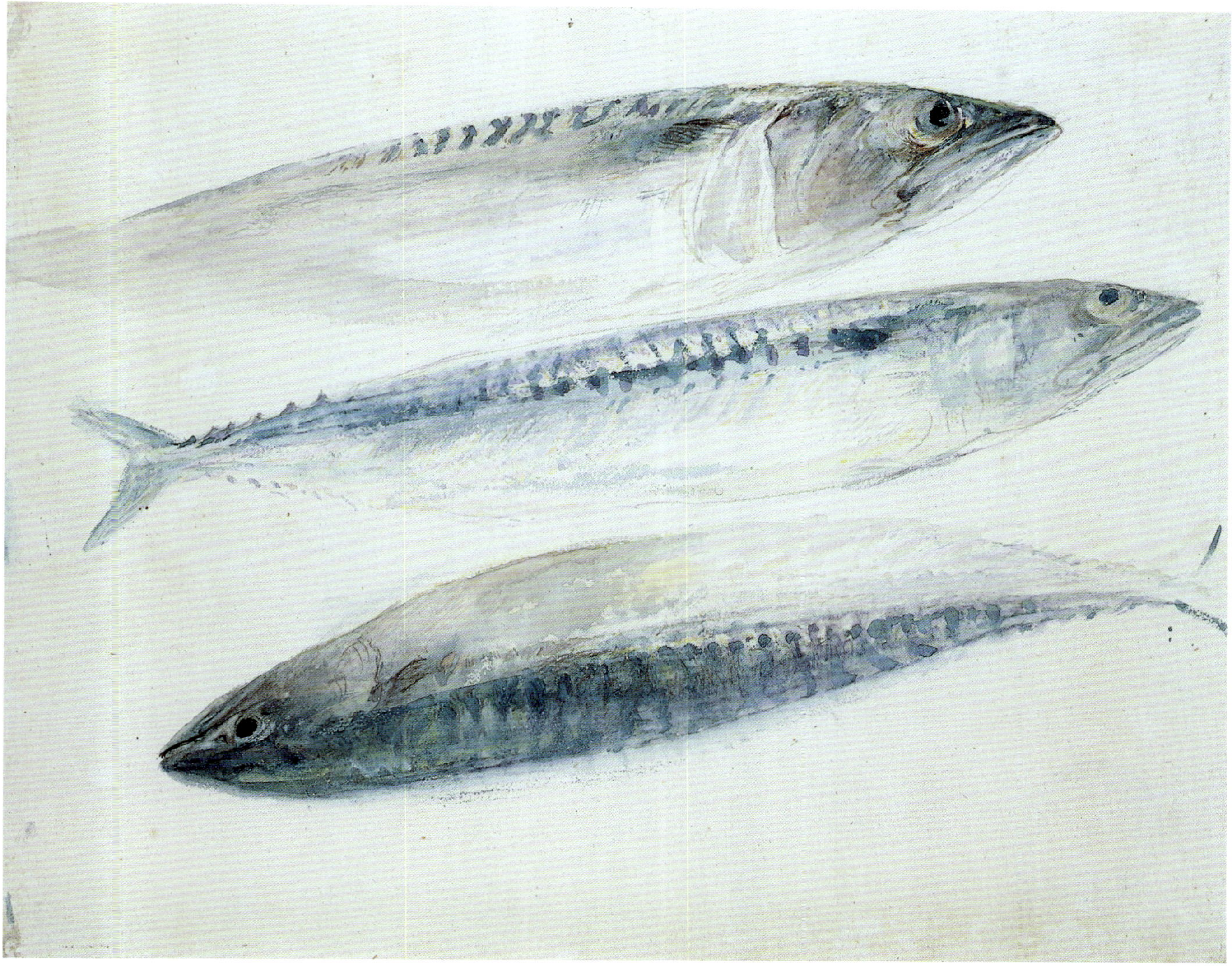

22 *Yarmouth, Norfolk*

watercolours over slight indications in pencil, with some scratching out, 24.2 × 35.8 cm
Presented by John Ruskin, 1861 [1861.11]
Herrmann 23; Wilton 1405

In addition to the elaborately composed view engraved for the *England and Wales* series in 1829, Turner made at least six other watercolours of Yarmouth, all from the same sketchbook and all in his more informal style of the 1830s. Here, the steeple and lighthouse are visible in the background, with the vast expanse of sands in the foreground. Seagulls keep a careful eye on the catch in the net, while incidental details such as the smoke from a steamer and the sailing boats punctuate the curved strokes describing land and sea.

Turner achieved wholly different results in his two oil paintings of Yarmouth, exhibited in 1831 and 1840,[1] both illustrating the Manby apparatus, a system which fired a stone on the end of a length of rope to provide a lifeline for a ship in distress, accompanied by flares.

[1] Butlin & Joll 336, 387

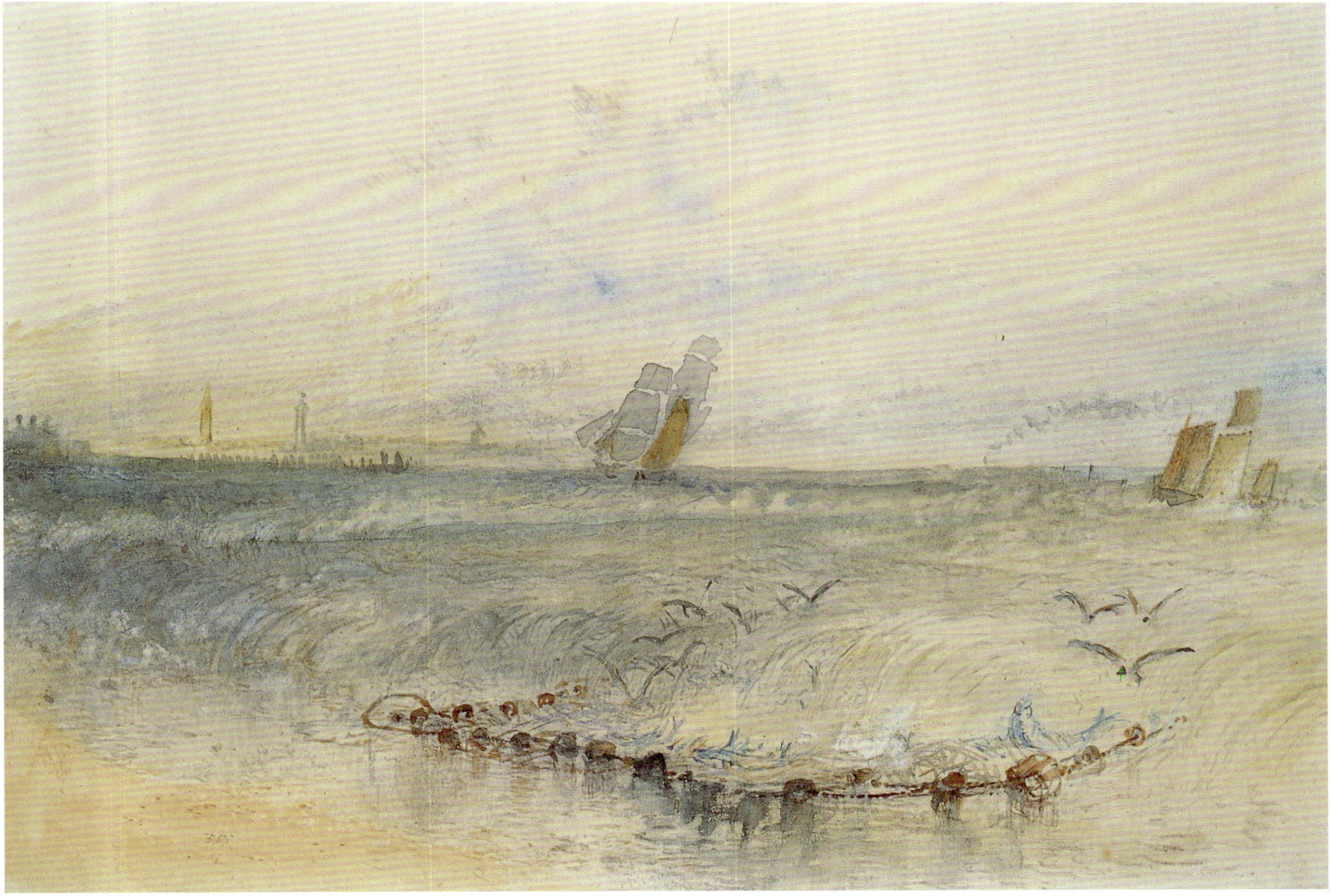

23 *Combe Martin, Devonshire*

watercolours over pencil, with pen and black ink, 14.6 × 23.2 cm
inscribed on the stern of the boat, *Combe Martin*
Presented by John Ruskin, 1861 [1861.5]
Herrmann 24; Wilton 476

In *c.*1811, the engraver and publisher, William Bernard Cooke, commissioned from Turner a series of watercolours to be published as *Picturesque Views on the Southern Coast of England*. Forty watercolours were engraved and appeared in parts between 1814 and 1826, for which the artist was paid ten guineas each, and the engraver 25. The locations chosen range from Whitstable in Kent to Watchet in Somerset, and, while Turner knew those in Kent and Sussex well, the views of the western counties were based on sketches made on new tours in 1811–14. Combe Martin is probably based on a sketch made on the first of these tours, recorded in the 'Devonshire Coast no. 1' sketchbook (T.B. CXXIII). The finished watercolour, which was engraved by William Miller and published in January 1825 (Rawlinson 119), was probably made in the previous year; Miller would have taken some months to complete the engraving. It seems probable that the artist himself proposed the alterations between the watercolour and the engraving, such as the addition of a sailing boat and masts.

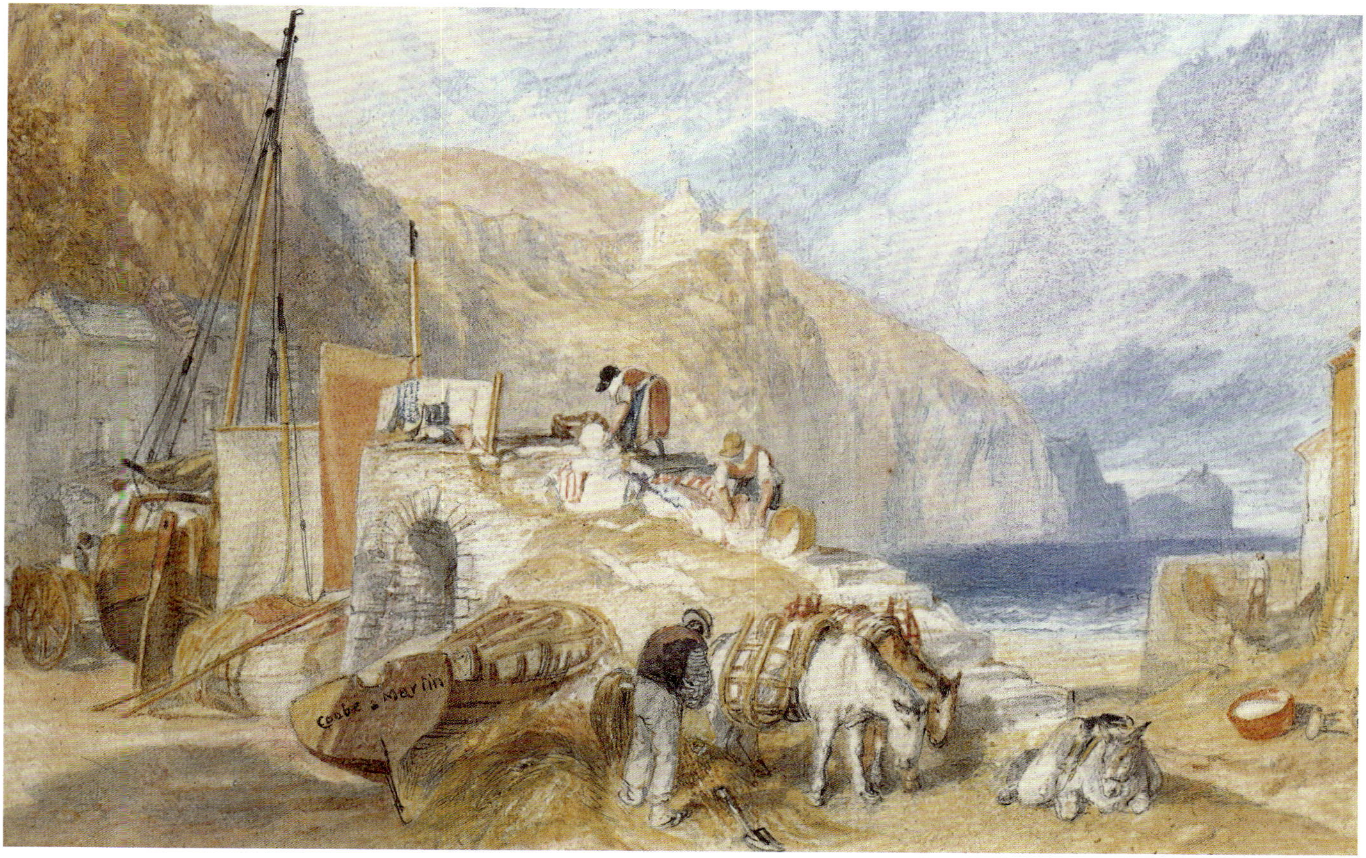

24 *Margate*

watercolours with scratching out, 15.4 × 25.5 cm
Presented by John Ruskin, 1861 [1861.7]
Herrmann 26; Wilton 757

This watercolour was probably made in the mid 1820s, when Turner was preoccupied with his work for the *The Picturesque Views on the Southern Coast of England* and the short-lived *Ports of England*, of which only six plates were published. It was eventually engraved in mezzotint by Thomas Lupton as one of 12 plates in *The Harbours of England*, which was published in 1856 with a text by Ruskin (Rawlinson 785). There, Ruskin noted that the drawing 'was left unfinished at his death, and I would not allow it to be touched afterwards, desiring that the series should remain as far as possible in an authentic state.' It shows a distant view of the port and seaside resort of Margate, with a paddle steamer in the harbour and bathing machines on the beach. In the middle distance, Turner shows the human struggle against the elements, as men try to recover the cargo of coal from a dismasted collier.

For Ruskin, this was not,

> at first sight, one of the most striking of the series; but it is very beautiful, and highly characteristic of Turner . . . if we enumerate the English ports one by one, from Berwick to Whitehaven, round the island, there will be hardly found another so utterly devoid of all picturesque or romantic interest as Margate. Nearly all have some steep eminence of down or cliff, some pretty retiring dingle, some roughness of old harbour or straggling fisher-hamlet, some fragment of castle or abbey on the heights above, capable of becoming a leading point in a picture; but Margate is simply a mass of modern parades and streets, with a little bit of chalk cliff, an orderly pier, and some bathing-machines. Turner never conceives it as anything else; and yet for the sake of this simple vision, again and again he quits all higher thoughts. (*Works*, XIII, p. 60)

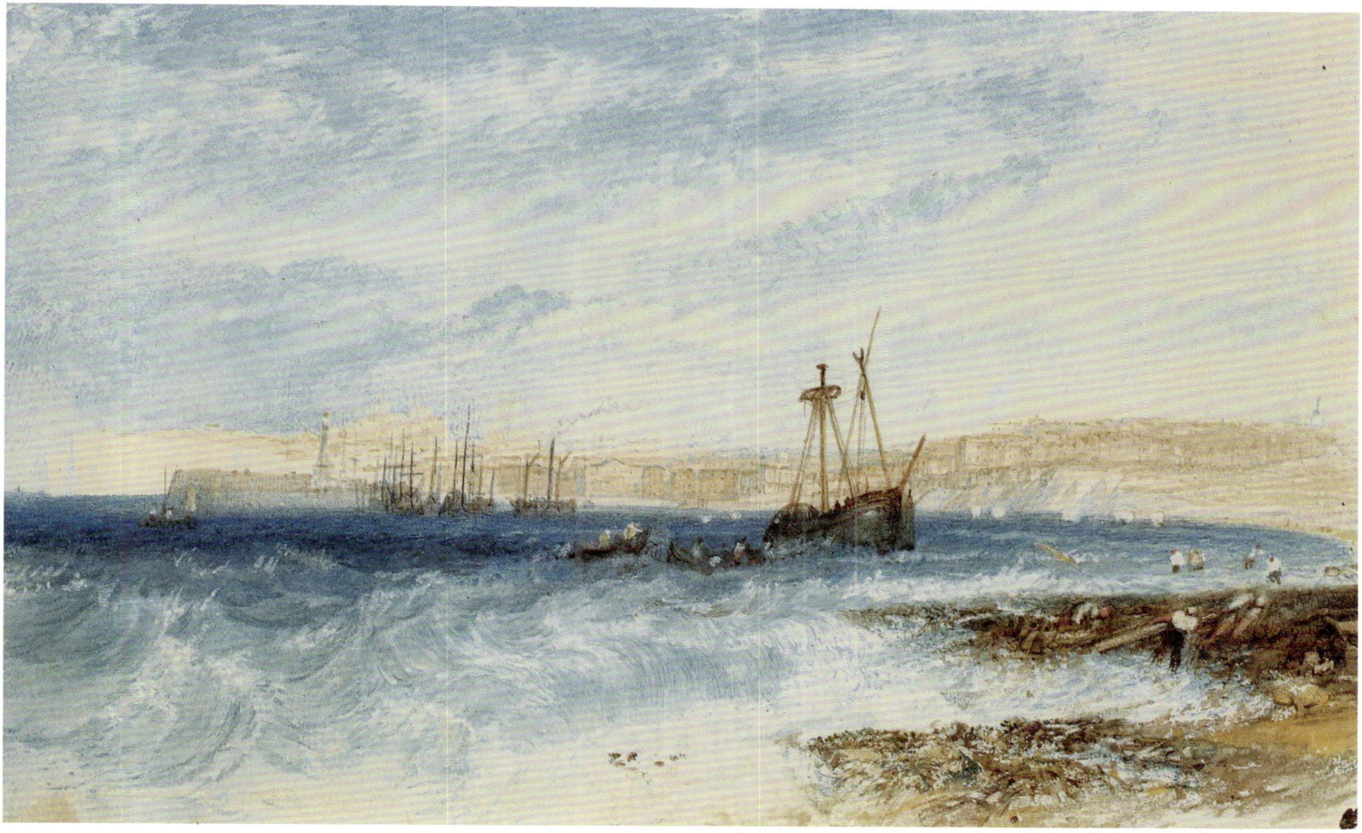

25 *Scene on the Loire, near the Coteaux de Mauves*

watercolours and body colours touched with pen and black ink, on blue paper faded to grey, 14 × 18.9 cm
Presented by John Ruskin, 1861 [1861.23]
Herrmann 50; Wilton 947

During the late 1820s, Turner repeatedly visited the Continent in connexion with the proposed publication of the *Great Rivers of Europe*, announced by Charles Heath in 1833, of which *The Rivers of France* appeared in three parts between 1833 and 1835. In northern France, he travelled up the Loire and down the Seine; in Germany and Switzerland, along the banks of the Moselle and Meuse. The sketchbooks he filled formed the basis for the distinctive series of watercolours on small, roughly torn, pieces of blue paper. Most are in body colour, an opaque medium Turner had begun using some years earlier.

Turner began the first of the tours in August 1826, when he set out from London, made a rapid circuit of the French coast from Dieppe round to the mouth of the Loire at Nantes, and more leisurely progress up the Loire as far as Orleans, where he arrived in the second week of October. On his journey, he stopped at several of the most celebrated monuments in France, the mediaeval cathedrals at Angers and Tours, the Renaissance chateaux of Blois and Beaugency, and Amboise. However, his journey was entirely purposeful, and he never allowed himself a detour to other places a little farther from the river banks.

From Nantes, Turner travelled upstream, probably by steamer, as far as Angers, when he took to the road. The steep rocky banks around Mauves-sur-Loire provided him with four watercolours for the Loire series, including this drawing, which was not engraved, but which Ruskin unequivocally described as 'the best of the Loire series', 'priceless'.

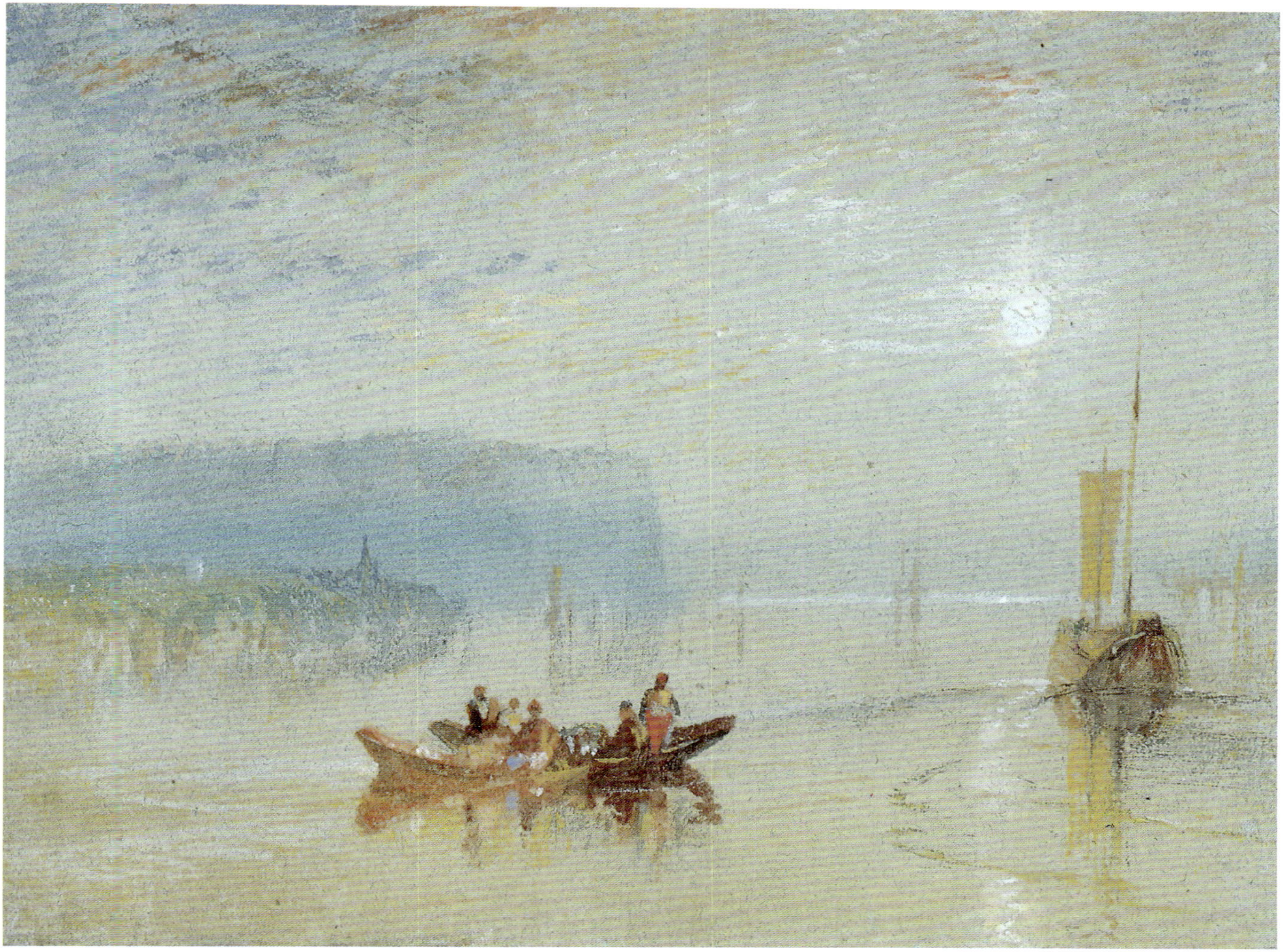

26 *Rietz, near Saumur*

watercolours and body colours over pencil, with pen and brown ink, on grey paper, 12.4 × 18.1 cm
Presented by John Ruskin, 1861 [1861.31]
Herrmann 49; Wilton 942

Between Saumur and Tours, Turner was detained only by the small villages of Montsoreau and Candes St Martin. The traditional title for this work stems from the old name for Montsoreau, Rets, whose distinctive church and castle are outlined here. The sunlight falls exactly on the point where the rivers merge at the confluence of the Loire and Vienne.

In *Modern Painters*, Ruskin described the scene thus:

> [The river banks] are excavated by the peasantry . . . and thus a kind of continuous village runs along the river-side, composed half of caves, half of rude buildings, backed by the cliff, propped against it, therefore always leaning away from the river; mingled with overlappings of vineyard trellis from above, when the grapes are ripe, or for gossip over the garden wall.
>
> It is an autumnal evening, then, by this Loire side. The day has been hot, and the air is heavy and misty still; the sunlight warm, but dim; the brown vine-leaves motionless: all else quiet. Not a sail in sight on the river, its strong noiseless current lengthening the stream of low sunlight.
>
> The motive of the picture, therefore, is the expression of rude but perfect peace, slightly mingled with an indolent langour and despondency; the space between intervals of enforced labour; happy, but listless, and having little care or hope about the future; cutting its home out of this gravel bank, and letting the vine and the river twine and undermine as they will; careless to mend or build, so long as the walls hold together, and the black fruit swells in the sunshine.
> (*Works*, VII, pp. 218–9)

This drawing was engraved by R. Brandard for *Turner's Annual Tour or Wanderings on the Loire*, 1833 (Rawlinson 444).

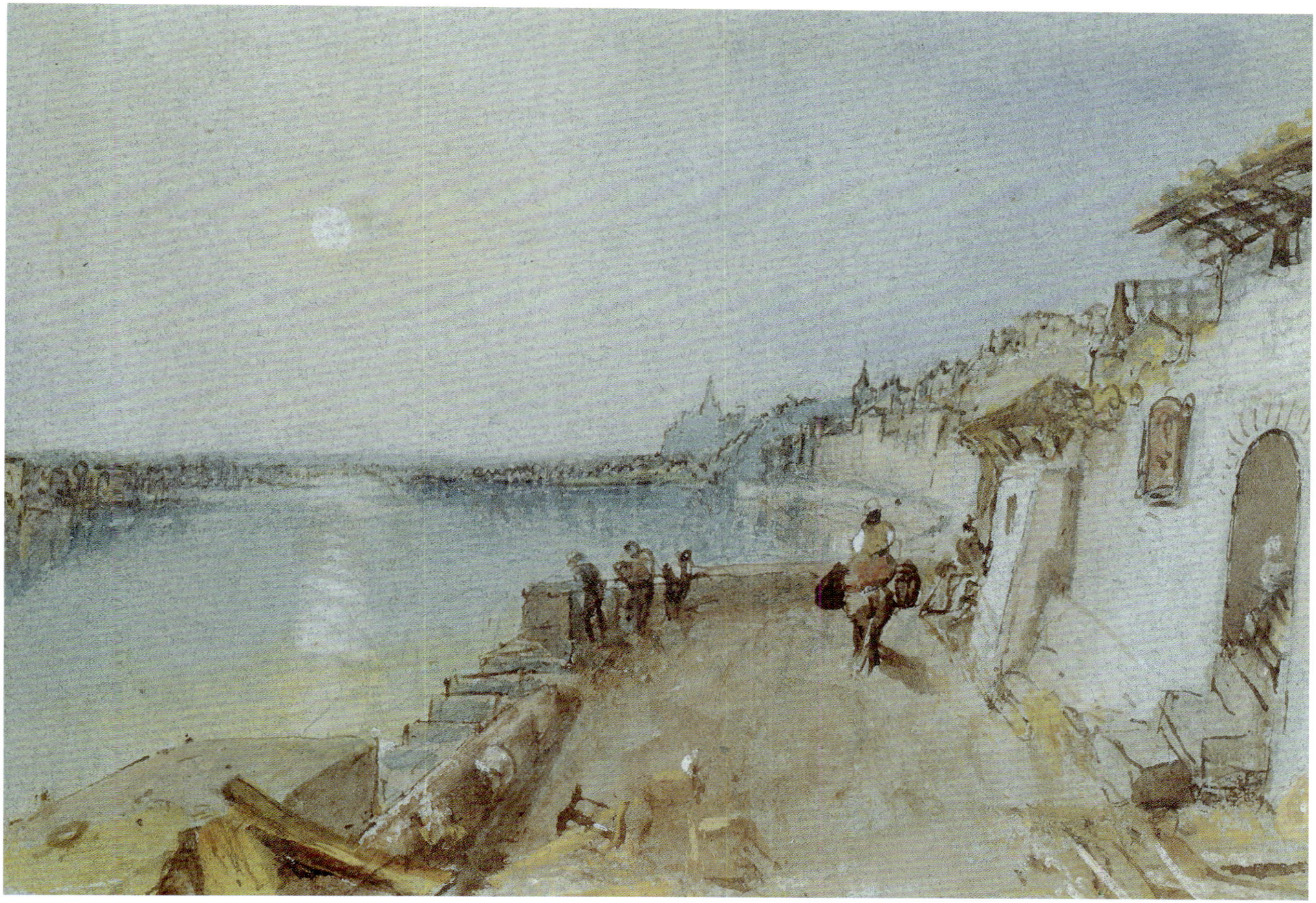

27 *Château of Amboise*

watercolours and body colours with pen and black ink, on grey paper, 13.6 × 18.8 cm
Presented by John Ruskin, 1861 [1861.28]
Herrmann 35; Wilton 936

At Amboise, Turner apparently devoted only one opening of his sketch-book to the chateau, bridge and five small general views. The three watercolours he developed are all in the Ashmolean: one shows Amboise from the west; another, the castle by moonlight; and the third, this imposing view of the fortress towering over the bridge, with the town appearing through one of the arches. It was engraved by James Bayliss Allen for *Turner's Annual Tour – The Loire* in 1833 (Rawlinson 438).

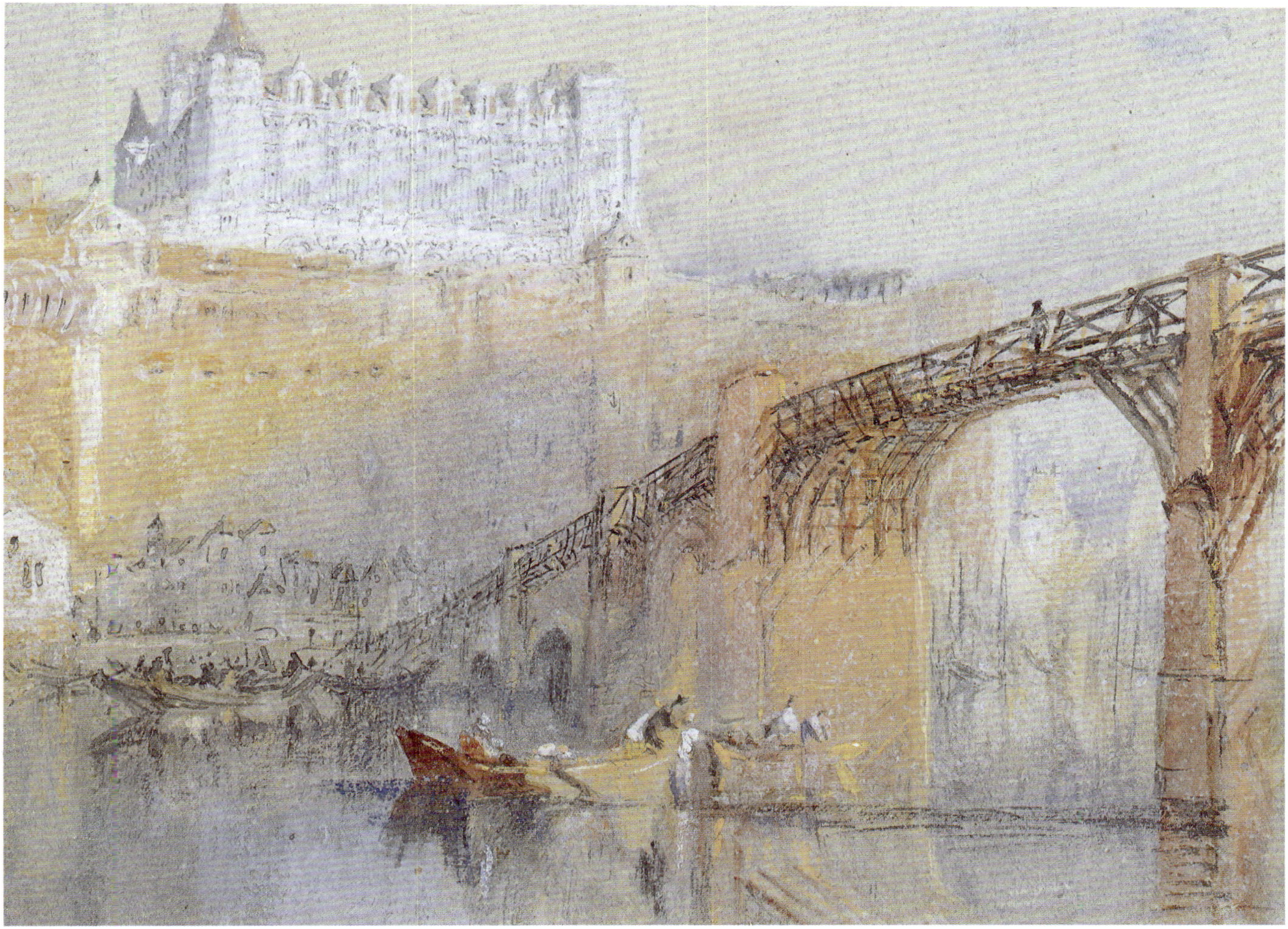

28 *Blois*

watercolours and body colours, with pen and brown and black inks, on grey paper, 13.5 × 18.3 cm
Presented by John Ruskin, 1861 [1861.32]
Herrmann 42; Wilton 933

Having spent perhaps only a single night at Amboise, Turner proceeded to Blois, where his pencil sketches provided him with material for four watercolours, two of which were engraved in *Turner's Annual Tour*, including this one, by R. Brandard (Rawlinson 435). Here, the town is seen from the western approaches along the river, a subject Turner had already made as a copy in the 1790s. The main quarter is visible on the left, with the façade of the château in white, the towers and spire of St Laumer outlined in brown ink, and the cathedral of Saint Louis and bishop's palace atop the hill. Jacques-Ange Gabriel's elegant bridge leads to the church of Saint Saturnin and the quartier de Vienne on the right. In the foreground, two figures sit watching the activities of boatmen, and a heavily laden donkey leads us into the composition, much as it had done in no. 26.

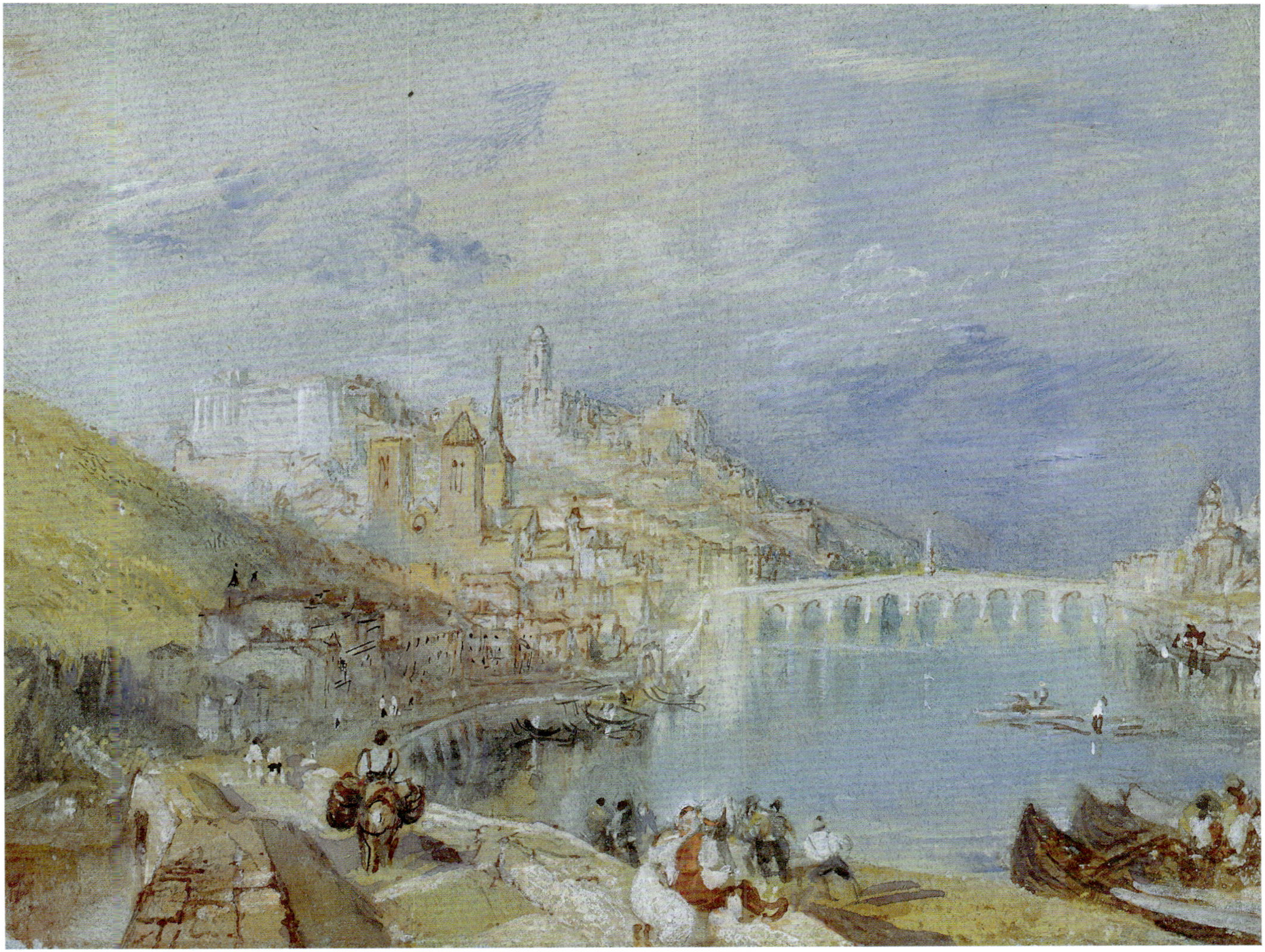

29 *Orleans*

watercolours and body colours with pen and red, brown and black inks, on blue paper faded to grey, 13.6 × 18.9 cm
Presented by John Ruskin, 1861 [1861.35]
Herrmann 48; Wilton 931

From Blois, Turner moved up river to Beaugency and thence to Orleans, where his pencil sketches provided him with nine colour views, four distant, and three concentrating on the western façade of the cathedral. As Turner would no doubt have known, this had only been completed recently, and is an intriguing mixture of gothic, and strict and square classicism. This view is taken from place de l'Etape, and shows the theatre and Hôtel Dieu from near the Hôtel Groslot. A carriage and procession enliven the scene.

Orleans was engraved by Thomas Higham for *Turner's Annual Tour – The Loire* in 1833 (Rawlinson 433).

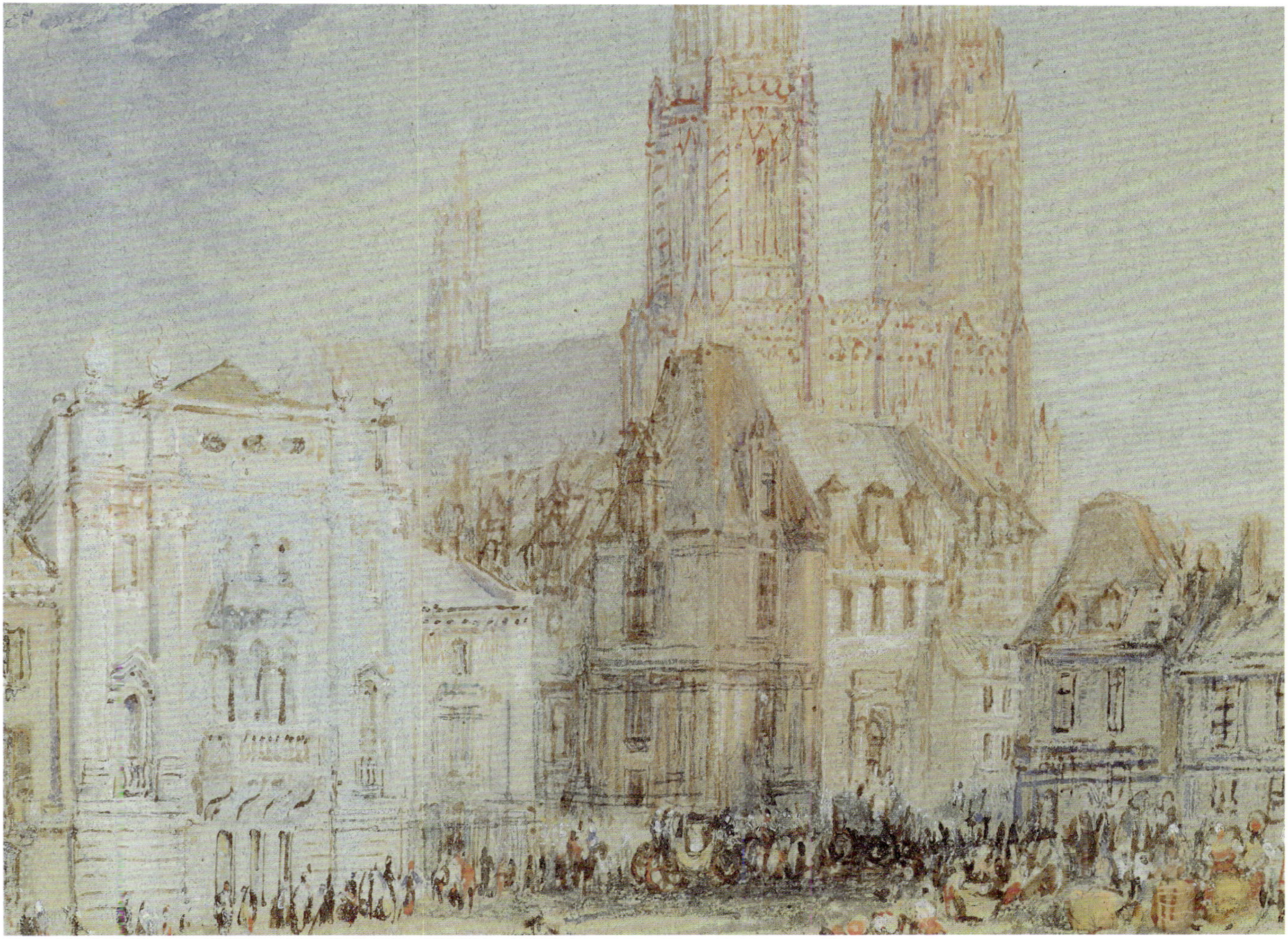

30 *Jericho*

watercolours over pencil, with pen and some scratching out, 12.2 × 19.8 cm
Prov.: J. F. Lewis
Presented by John Ruskin, 1861 [1861.4]
Herrmann 55; Wilton 1240

Unlike many of his contemporaries, Turner was never tempted to visit the Near East, and his set of watercolours engraved for *The Biblical Keepsake, or Landscape Illustrations of the most remarkable Places mentioned in the Holy Scriptures* (1835), was based on sketches made by various artists, notably Sir Charles Barry, who had been in the Levant between 1817 and 1820. *Jericho* was based on a sketch by the Revd R. Masters, and engraved by William Finden (Rawlinson 576).

Ruskin paid 90 guineas for this watercolour, which he believed to be an 'entirely first-rater' (*Works*, XXXVI, pp. 358–9). He exchanged it with the painter, J. F. Lewis, in 1858, for two of Lewis's own sketches, but bought it back in the following year.

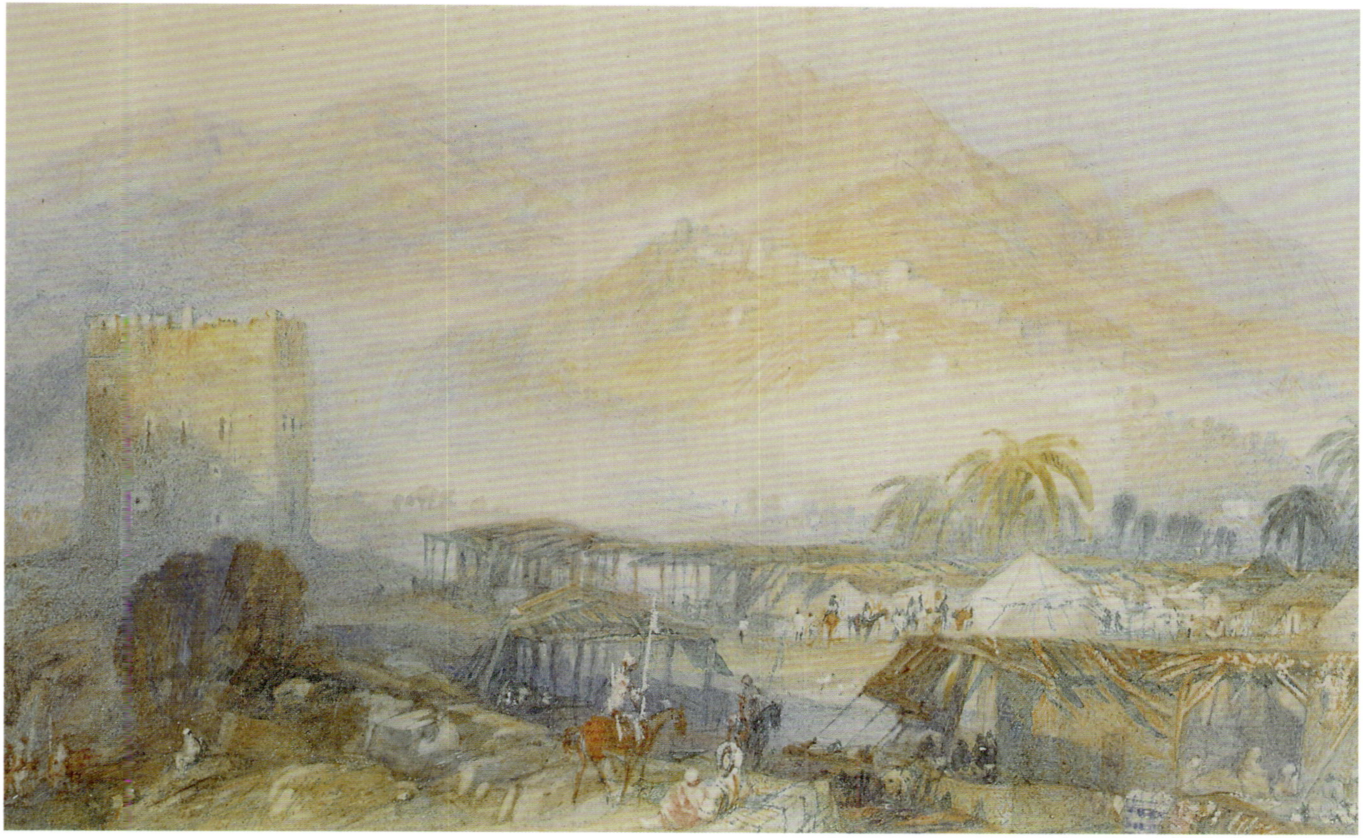

31 *Scene on the Moselle: Alf and Burg Arras*

watercolours and body colours, with pen and reddish and brown inks, on grey paper, 13.4 × 18.6 cm
Presented by John Ruskin, 1861 [1861.14]
Herrmann 27; Wilton 1023; Powell 61

Until recently, this watercolour was known as a scene on the Meuse, and associated with one of Turner's tours in France. However, as discovered by Cecilia Powell, it in fact shows the village of Alf, on the Moselle, with the tributary of the Alf running into it under the bridge. Behind is the ruined tower of Burg Arras, while in the foreground, the villagers busy themselves at the water's edge.

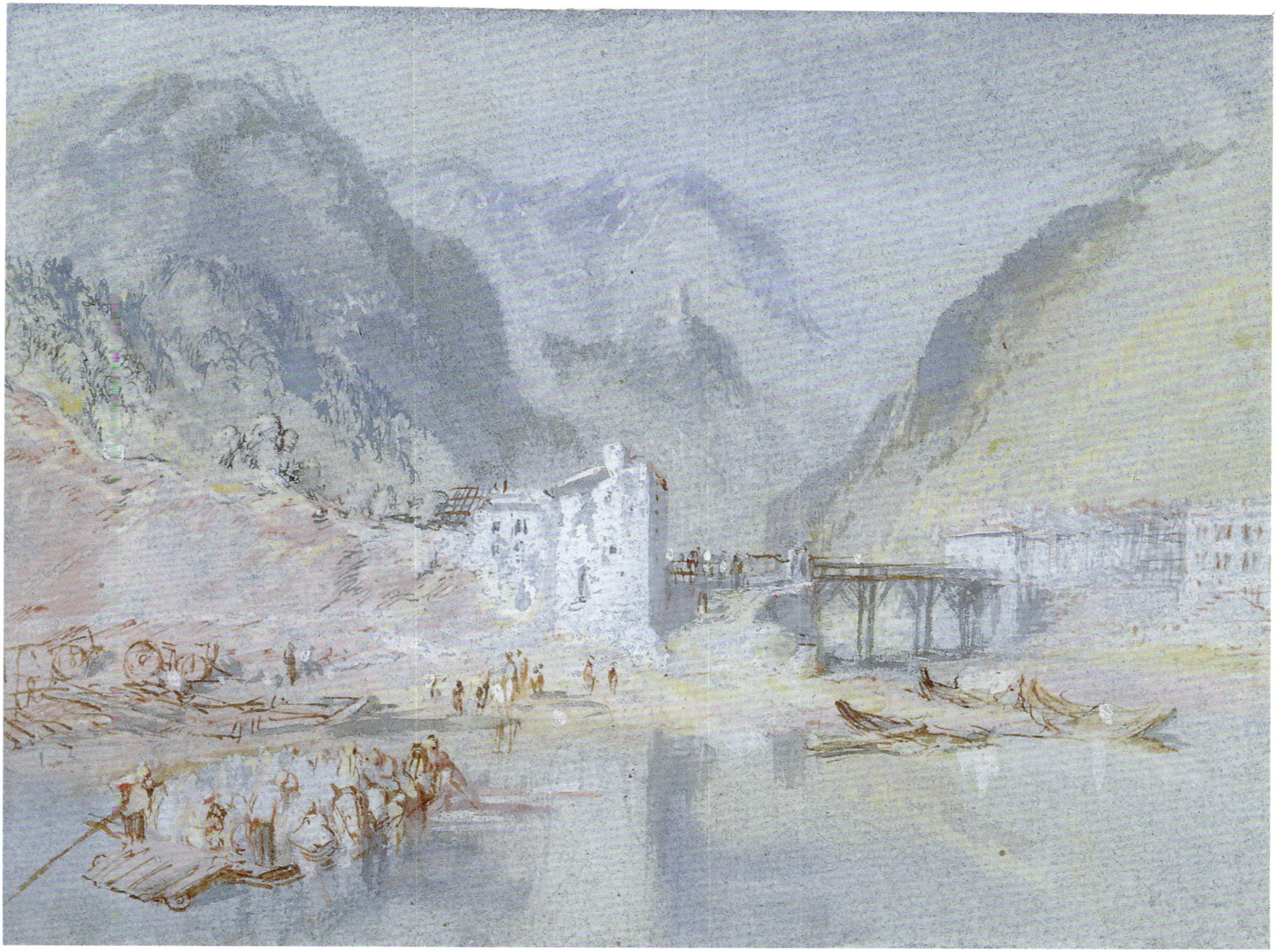

32 *Venice: The Grand Canal*

watercolours over pencil with pen and red and blue inks and white body colour, 21.5 × 31.5 cm
Presented by John Ruskin, 1861 [1861.8]
Herrmann 56; Wilton 1363

On his third and last trip to Venice, Turner left London at the end of July, 1840, and arrived on 20 August, according to the local newspaper. He remained about a fortnight, and returned via Trieste and central Germany on 7 October. William Callow, also a visitor at the same time, remembered that, 'one evening whilst I was enjoying a cigar in a gondola I saw in another one Turner sketching San Giorgio, brilliantly lit up by the setting sun. I felt quite ashamed of myself idling away the time whilst he was hard at work so late' (quoted in Stainton, p. 22).

The three views of Venice in the Ashmolean all date from Turner's last visit to the city in 1840, and were probably extracted from the same roll-sketchbook. Ruskin presented a further three to the Fitzwilliam Museum in Cambridge. The view of the Grand Canal is taken looking towards Santa Maria della Salute, from mid-stream near the Accademia, where the hideous bridge was put up in 1854. The architecture on the left is drawn in a complicated network of red, blue and black inks with scratching out with a blunt point; their reflections washed in violet, blue and pink.

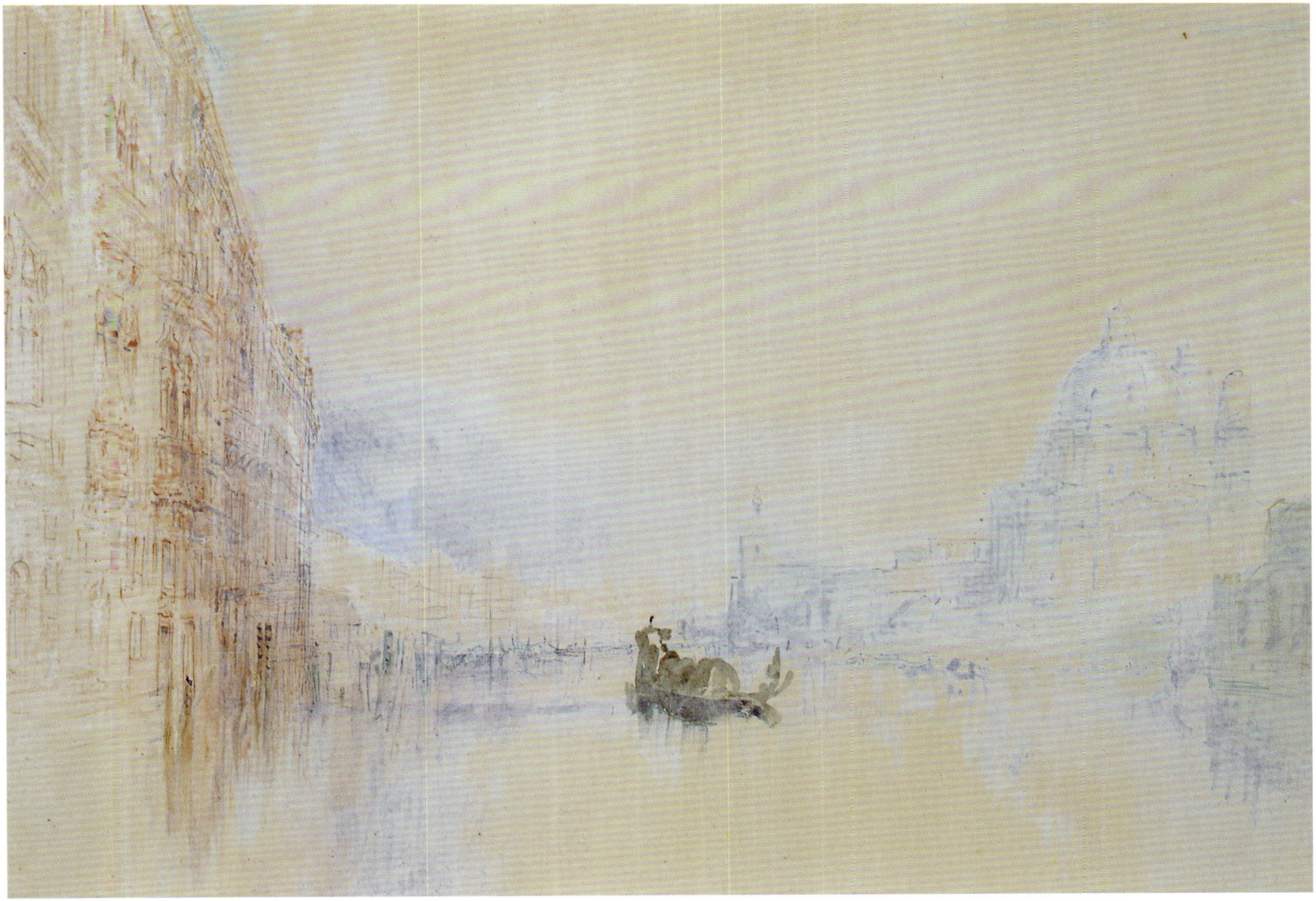

watercolours over pencil with pen and red and black inks, and some scraping out, 21.7 × 31.8 cm
Presented by John Ruskin, 1861 [1861.9]
Herrmann 57; Wilton 1366

The Accademia delle Belle Arti was established in its present accomoda-tion, the former convent of the Carità, by the French administration in 1807, when the present neo-classical facade was erected. Turner seems not to have visited the picture gallery, but its exterior inspired him to one of his most balanced and poetic designs.

In his *Guide to the Principal Pictures in the Academy of Fine Arts at Venice*, 1877, Ruskin described this work as 'Turner's lovely sketch [of the Accademia] painted as he saw it fifty years ago, with bright golden sails grouped in front of it where now is the ghastly iron bridge.' The bridge was replaced in 1932 by a temporary wooden structure which still stands and is scarcely less ugly than its predecessor.

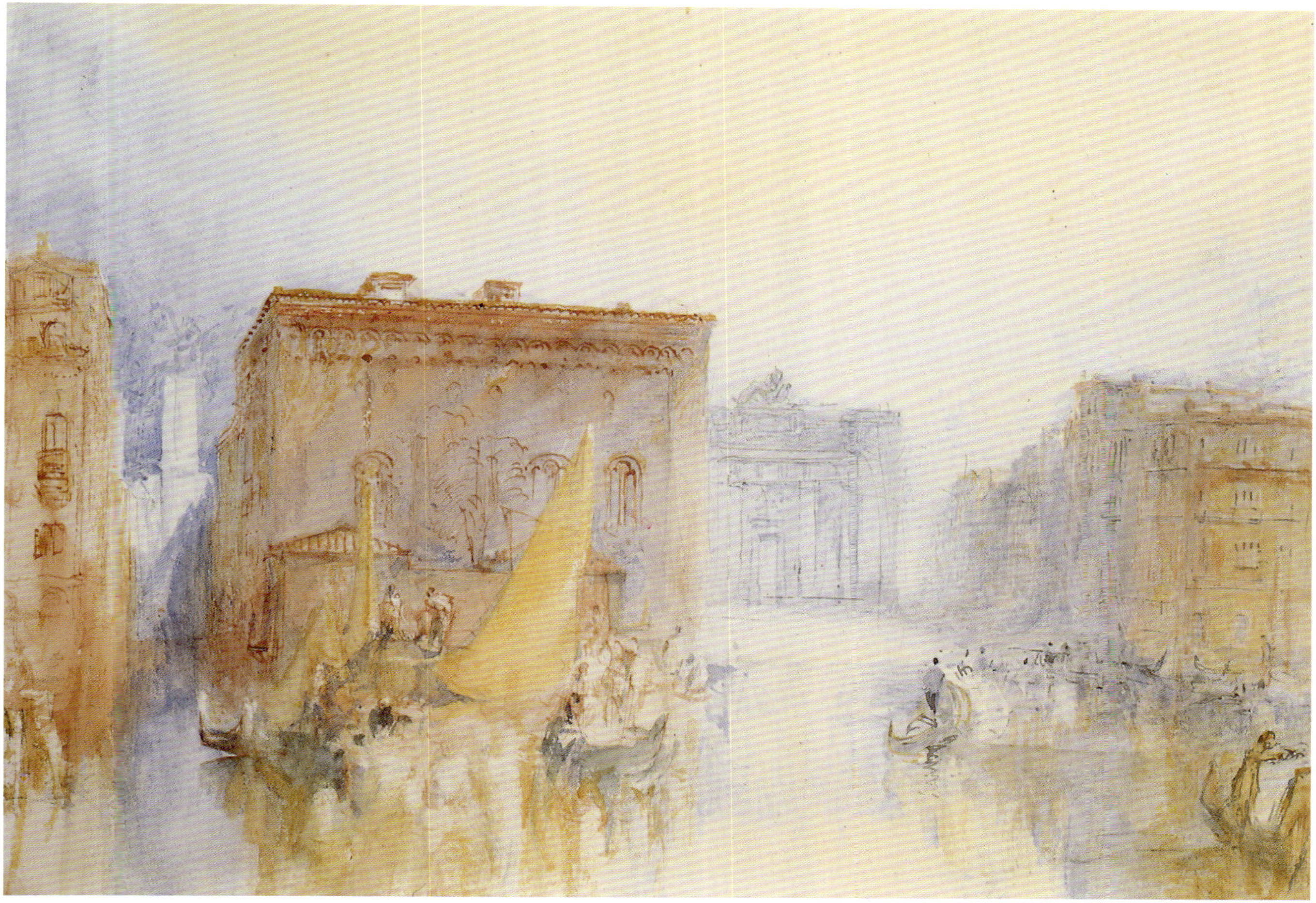

34 *Evening: Cloud on Mount Rigi, seen from Zug*

watercolours, 21.8 × 26.7 cm
Ruskin School Collection (Educational Series, no. 300)
Herrmann 86; Wilton 1474

After his first trip to Switzerland in 1802, Turner did not return until the mid-1830s. Between 1841 and 1844, however, he made an annual tour. The numerous sketches and watercolours he made on these later visits are difficult to date, and many of the motifs recur in different years. One of his favourite views was from the Swan Inn at Lucerne, where he stayed, looking over the lake towards the dominant and eccentric form of Mount Rigi. On his return to England in 1842, he included three views of the Rigi among the ten magnificent works sold through his new dealer, Thomas Griffith of Norwood. Turner's old friend, Munro of Novar, bought two of the views of Rigi (and five other watercolours besides), and Ruskin, two of the set. However, Ruskin prized even more the watercolour studies made on the spot: 'I understand the meaning of these sketches – and I can work them up into pictures in my head – and reason out a great deal of the man from them which I cannot from the drawings'.

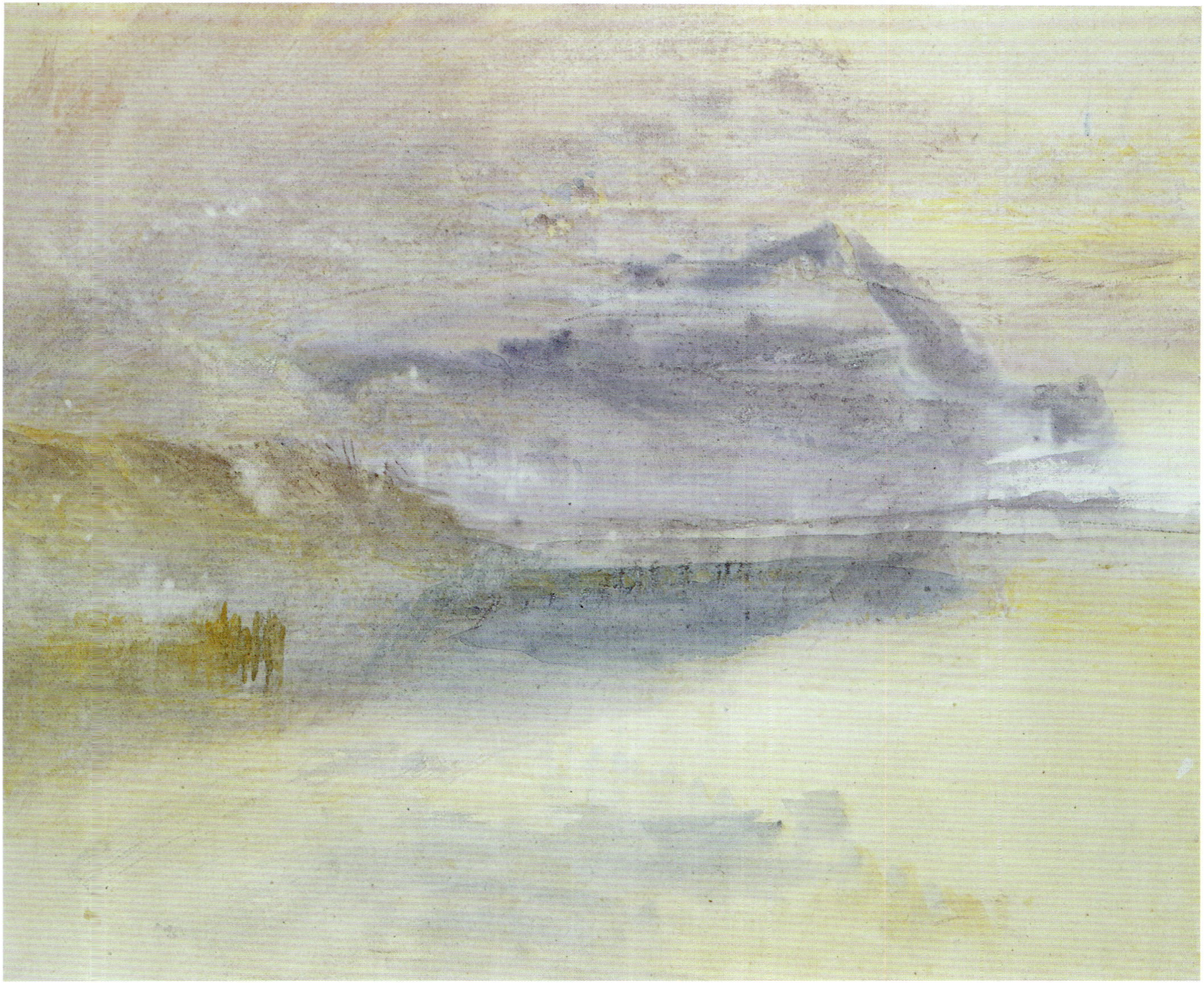

Further reading

The literature on Turner is vast and, after the opening of the Clore Gallery at the Tate Gallery, in belated fulfilment of the intentions of his will, has increased considerably in recent years. The fundamental source for the works in the Ashmolean is **Luke Herrmann**, *Ruskin and Turner* (London, 1968). Among other books, the following are essential:

W. Thornbury *The Life of J. M. W. Turner, R.A.* (London, 1862; rev. edn, 1876)
A. J. Finberg *The Life of J. M. W. Turner, R.A.* (Oxford, 1939; rev. edn, 1961)
James Hamilton *Turner, A Life* (London, 1997)
W. G. Rawlinson *The Engraved Work of J. M. W. Turner, R.A.* (London, 1908, 1913)
A. J. Finberg *The History of Turner's 'Liber Studiorum' with a new Catalogue raisonné* (London, 1924)
Martin Butlin and Evelyn Joll *The Paintings of J. M. W. Turner*, 2 vols (New Haven and London, 1979; rev. edn, 1984)
Andrew Wilton *The Life and Work of J. M. W. Turner* (London, 1979) [includes a catalogue of the watercolours and summary catalogue of the oil paintings derived from Butlin and Joll)
Collected Correspondence of J. M. W. Turner, ed. John Gage (Oxford, 1980)
John Gage *J. M. W. Turner: 'A Wonderful Range of Mind'* (New Haven and London, 1987)
John Ruskin *Works*, ed E. T. Cook and Alexander Wedderburn, 39 vols (London, 1903–12), especially vol. XIII

On specific aspects of works illustrated in this handbook, see:

Luke Herrmann 'Ruskin and Turner: A riddle solved', *Burlington Magazine*, CXII (1970), pp. 696–9
Helen Mary Petter *The Oxford Almanacks* (Oxford, 1974)
Malcolm Cormack *J. M. W. Turner, R.A. 1775–1851: A Catalogue of the Drawings and Watercolours in the Fitzwilliam Museum, Cambridge* (Cambridge, 1975)
Francina Irwin *et al.* *Turner in Scotland* (exh. cat., Aberdeen Art Gallery, 1982)
Andrew Wilton *Turner in Wales* (exh. cat., Mostyn Art Gallery, Llandudno and Glynn Vivian Art Gallery and Museum, Swansea, 1984)
Patrick Youngblood 'The Stones of Oxford: Turner's Depiction of Oxonian Architecture', *Turner Studies*, vol. 3, no. 2 (1984), pp. 3–21
Lindsay Stainton *Turner's Venice* (London, 1985)
Luke Herrmann *Turner Prints: The Engraved Work of J. M. W. Turner* (Oxford, 1990)
Cecilia Powell *Turner's Rivers of Europe: The Rhine, Meuse and Mosel* (exh. cat., Tate Gallery, London, 1991)
Gillian Forrester *Turner's 'Drawing Book': The Liber Studiorum* (exh. cat., Tate Gallery, London, 1996)
Ian Warrell *Turner on the Loire* (exh. cat., Tate Gallery, London, 1997)